Systemic and Borderline
Banking Crises

Lessons Learned for Future Prevention

Irakli Kovzanadze

iUniverse, Inc.
New York   Bloomington

Systemic and Borderline Banking Crises
Lessons Learned for Future Prevention

iUniverse books may be ordered through booksellers or by contacting:

iUniverse
1663 Liberty Drive
Bloomington, IN 47403
www.iuniverse.com
1-800-Authors (1-800-288-4677)

ISBN: 978-1-4502-3060-5 (pbk)
ISBN: 978-1-4502-3062-9 (cloth)
ISBN: 978-1-4502-3061-2 (ebk)

Printed in the United States of America

iUniverse rev. date: 11/1/2010

Contents

Introduction

Globalisation involves many spheres of human existence and "financial globalisation" is one of the most integral component parts of this ongoing process.

The end of the 20th and the beginning of the 21st centuries are characterised by the "firework" show that has been witnessed by an increase in inherent instability in the sphere of international development. In response, economists are trying to understand the causes and effects as they seek better ways to overcome intrinsic problems.

Using a strategy of immersed research in addressing these issues, starting out with an understanding of the genesis and growth of systemic banking crises in many countries, they continue their quest by addressing such issues with tools that allow for a comprehensive analysis in reaching relevant and timely conclusions.

This summary work across regions and countries is presented as a comprehensive analysis of both the theoretical and practical approaches, and also addresses the causes and progression of banking crises, and what is even more important in their forecasting and prevention.

Based on a broad based exemplary foundation, classified systemic banking crises are further classified and explained within theories of their genesis, with attention on macroeconomic, structural and institutional factors.

Special emphasis is placed on the restructuring of the given banking system when talking about overcoming a systemic banking crisis and the effort focuses on regulatory and supervisory control in overcoming crises.

Examples and analysis in the work are taken from the comprehensive research material on the subject that is reflective of the experience of different countries and regions of the world. True, special attention is paid to the banking problems in Georgia in the book, the mechanisms of their development and the ways to prevent such crises.

If anything, modern economic literature is not lacking in terms of how to deal with issues of financial globalisation and banking crises. However, this book provides a unique opportunity to become better acquainted with the most up to date information on a very sultry problem at hand and affords rich "food" for further reflection. Nevertheless, the book does not formally represent a textbook in the traditional meaning, rather it should be considered as a particularly useful manuscript that graduate, post-graduate students and lecturers can use as a resource material in familiarising themselves with the subject during the course of their continued study of economics.

CHAPTER 1
Genesis of systemic banking crises

1.1. Systemic banking crisis: types and forms of manifestation

Two associated trends can be noted in the development of the world's economy: globalisation and growth of instability. These have been evidently noticeable in the last two decades and such trends are especially conspicuous in the banking sector because of its extreme sensitivity to a number of external influences.

Negative external influence conjoined with structural imbalances in the economy and the banking sector in the presence of inadequate institutional infrastructure led to the systemic banking crisis which had become a common occurrence in the last two decades of the 20th century in the world.

The research presented herein seeks to provide alternative reasons why the banking crisis came about by identifying and analysing the contributing factors and characteristics of the crisis.

According to the opinion of professors M. Shaffer and R. Mokri from the University of Harriett-Watt (Edinburgh), the systemic banking crisis is characterised by an increase in the share of bad and uncollected debts that exist in bank credit portfolios. Consequently many banks, not just the well publicised "problem banks", are experiencing difficulties such as poor liquidity.

Various researchers, such as Jeffrey J. Sacks, director of the Harvard Institute of International Development, and P. Walker another American economist both note that a systemic banking crisis manifests itself in financial panic, characterised by runs on banks caused by depositors hastily withdrawing their money. The well-known researchers of systemic crises, F. Allen of Pennsylvanian University and D. Gale of New-York University, share the same opinion.

Many economists pay attention to other signs of the systemic crisis, such as the destabilisation of the situation on inter-bank markets and the problems with clearing operations. At the same time, as noted in various research studies, macro-economic imbalance is realised in the form of inflation and, in extreme cases, *hyper*-inflation, coupled with a sharp increase in credit needs and the effects of economic recession becoming noticeable.

By analysing a number of the characteristic features and forms of the manifestation of the systemic banking crisis, it would be reasonable to consider that much of the problem can be explained as a rapid and large-scale deterioration of the quality of the banking assets which results from adverse macro-economic, institutional and regulatory factors. A systemic banking crisis shows up in the inability of a significant number of credit institutions (and, often, the banking system as a whole) to perform basic functions such as settlement operations and the transformation of savings into investments, with the crisis then compounded by panic among the bank's creditors, primarily amongst its depositors, and a collapse of the inter-bank credits market.

Banking collapse caused enormous economic and social damage in the 19th century; however, western countries faced The Great Depression as recently as the 1930s. The problems in the banking sector then were the consequences and the part of the pervasive crisis of the economy, social and political institutions. To overcome the situation and to avoid the emergence of systemic banking crises in the future, the developed countries adopted a complex regulatory system, which incorporated a special legislative framework to regulate banking activities. Firstly, in order to address issues of bankruptcy and the liquidation of banks, supervisory authorities aimed at reducing the risk of the bank transactions, partly by means of limiting competition. The institute of the "lender of last resort was set up to deal with critical situations", i.e. a special financial body (for example, the Central Bank), having sufficient funds and relevant powers of authority to intervene in the activities of various banks to either prevent or overcome a crisis. The regulatory system that was instigated in the 1930s and 1940s sought to protect the developed countries from the serious problems in the banking sector of the economy and continued to be effective to the 1970s and the early 1980s.

However, as a result of the growth of instability by the end of the 1970s there has since been a number of systemic banking crisis that occurred in more than 70 countries worldwide. These have affected both developed and developing countries and transitional economies. In some countries these crises have occurred on several occasions.

The systemic banking crises occurred in the following developed countries: the United States (1984-1991), Japan (1995), France (1994-1995), Spain (1977-1985), Austria (1989-1990), Norway (1987-1989), Sweden (1991), Finland (1991-1994), New Zealand (1987-1990), Australia (1989-1992), South Korea (1997), Turkey (1982-1985, 2000-2003), Israel (1977-1983), Great Britain (1974-1976), Germany (1970s), Denmark (198701992), Canada (1983-1985), Greece (1991-1995), Italy (1990-1995), Iceland (1985-1986).

Developing countries are especially prone to these kind of crises, where the problems of adaptation to globalisation and the growth of the financial instability are combined with so called "growth problems" (i.e. where legislation and institutional transformation lag behind social and economic changes, there is a weakening among state institutions and an increasingly excessive role played by foreign capital, including aspects of speculative dealings, etc.).

For example, destructive systemic banking crises affected most of Latin America, in some of them the crises occurred more than once, thus endangering not only the national economy but also the social-political situation within the country. In the case of Argentina, crisis situations were noticeable during the periods spanning 1980-1982, 1989-1990, and 1994-1995. In 2000 the following systemic banking crisis started in Argentina, a crisis which has still not been overcome. Crises occurred in Brazil three times: in 1990, in 1994 and again in 2000-2003. Very similar crises occurred three times in Costa Rica and Mexico whereas Venezuela and Chile faced a crisis on two separate occasions.

In the 1980s and 1990s two waves of crises swept past the countries of South-East Asia. However, the crisis of the late 1990s was more serious because of its impact on the world's economy which led to talks about the inefficiency (and sometimes even simply bankruptcy) of the policy of the international financial institutes, particularly of the International Monetary Fund (IMF).

Serious problems were also experienced in the Chinese banking system in the 1990s.

Transitional countries have virtually all experienced systemic banking crises and these resulted from the problems of transition to a market-based economy and market-driven banking sector. However, the negative influence of financial globalisation is also rather evident in these countries. The banking crises in Russia (1998), in the Baltic countries (mid 1990s), Czech (1993-1995), and Bulgaria (1995-1997) were especially conspicuous in terms of their impact on the world economic order, and on the overall reputation of the International Monetary Fund (IMF.) The systemic banking crises affected virtually all former socialist countries in both the Soviet Union and Eastern Europe, for example Armenia (1994-1996), Croatia (1996), Georgia (1998), Hungary (1991-1995), Poland (the early 1990s) and Ukraine (1997-1998), amongst others.

There are different kinds of banking crises.

In terms of their consequences, the crises could be divided into:

- Crisis functioning on the micro-economic level;
- Crisis distributed at the macro-economic level;
- Crisis characterised by large-scale budgetary financial destabilisation and leading to high inflation and a demonetisation of the economy.

The crises in most of the developed countries, for example in the United States (1984-1991), Sweden (1990-1993), Finland (1991-1994), and France (1991-1998), had clear macro-economic roots. However, the bankruptcy of a particular number of banks did not infect the entire financial system and did not result in macro-economic imbalances in such cases.

For example, while restructuring the banking system in Sweden, and with emphasis on overcoming the acute phase of the crisis (the crisis of the banking liquidity), the Central Bank injected significant resources to assure the liquidity of the banking sector. However, the monetary authorities were soon able to skilfully neutralise and overcome the excess of the liquidity by issuing long-term commercial instruments to manage debt. Concurrently, in the process of the successful restructuring of the problem banks, it became possible to partly compensate for the incurred costs. As a result, and despite huge financial resources mobilised to overcome the crisis, there were no destabilising effects, either on the rate of inflation or on the budget sector in general.

The most representative example of a typical crisis, and its impact on the macro level, could be considered in the crises experienced by the countries of South-East Asia, and also by some of the countries in Latin America, e.g. in Chile. The combined losses of the economy and the banking sector in these countries were rather high. Therefore, the costs incurred by governments in overcoming the acute phase of the systemic crisis and in recapitalising the banking system were substantial. The price which the Chilean government paid to overcome the consequences of the crisis there is estimated as 42 percent of their GDP, in Indonesia the government paid 50-55 percent of their GDP, in South Korea it was 20 percent of their GDP, in Malaysia the figure was 21 percent and it was 42 percent of the GDP in Thailand. Such a form of a systemic banking crisis tends to impact economic activity, profit and production structure, as well as the level of employment. Concurrently, clear fiscal and financial policy of the monetary authorities of these countries allowed compensating to a great extent the negative macro-economic implications of the large-scale expenditure for the restructuring. As a result despite the fact that the funds allocated for restructuring have not been repaid, the economy experienced serious shocks. However, in the wake of this, it was possible to avoid significant macro-economic destabilisation.

Argentina is a vivid example of another type of systemic banking crisis that leads to full-scale fiscal destabilisation and accompanying high inflation and demonetisation of the economy. The crisis in this country brought about major weakening of the financial system and intensification of the rate of inflation, which in its turn, accounted for the development of two high inflationary crises: 1984-1986 and 1989-1991. In 2001-2002, a complete collapse of the economy was observed; the causes of the Argentinean crisis to a large extent could be explained by a combination of inadequate state policy of how to restructure the banking system, and dogmatic monetary policy.

A classical example of the open form of the crisis, which manifested itself in creditors and depositors' panic, the collapse of the settlement system and the introduction of "bank holidays", could be the situation in the United States in the period 1929-1933. Such characteristics have also been observed during crises in many developing countries, e.g. in Argentina, Brazil, and Indonesia.

In the modern developed countries, where there are effective deposit insurance systems and the Central Banks actively play the role of "the lender of last resort", the emergence of an open form of banking crisis is less likely. While the latent form of the crisis or the bank distress as is referred to in various foreign studies, is more likely to emerge. If this is the case, a significant number of the credit institutions could lose their capital, experience serious liquidity problems, i.e. to be a bankrupt de facto. However, as a result of "built-in stabilisers" of the banking system, the issue of insolvency of the banks *de jure* may depend on the actions of the monetary authorities, peculiarities of the national law, and political influence of the banking lobby, etc.

Systemic banking crises have a so called "contagious" character. Firstly, the problems in the economy and the banking sector of one country have direct implications on the banking system of another country. The so called "Tequila Effect" is widely known. This phrase was coined when the devaluation of the Mexican peso and the banking crisis in Mexico in 1994 led to the dramatic deterioration of the situation on the whole continent of Latin America as a result of panic among foreign creditors and investors, mainly those involved in activities of a speculative nature. The crisis in Argentina, Brazil, Uruguay and other countries, certainly, had internal causes. However, the deterioration of the situation further occurred as a result of regionalisation of the Mexican problems. The crisis in the Scandinavian countries, which happened at around the same time, although not to the same extent, had common causes and effects.

In other countries, for example in the US and France, their banking crises are attributed to causes, and at least partially, to the accumulation of structural imbalances within the banking, system coupled with shortcomings and failures of regulatory oversight.

A systemic banking crisis has the capacity to encompass all segments of the banking sector (all types of credit institutions independent of their ownership structure or organisational and legal form) and it can affect certain types of banking organisations in many ways. Take, for example, the banking crisis in the US where, in the 1980s, a large number of these credit institutions turned out to be insolvent, whereas the crisis in Argentina demonstrated insolvency of state, cooperative and private banks.

The more serious consequences of a banking crisis can also be staved off on a local basis. In some of the countries, despite the serious problems experienced by the banking system as a whole, not all regions were affected, so while crises may have some common features, they also often expose strongly pronounced national peculiarities.

1.2. Systemic banking crisis as a result of combined impact of systemic banking risks

Despite their diversity, systemic banking crises most definitely have common causes, and understanding these is essential in perceiving the nature of these systemic banking risks.

Risks are often reflected by a situational characteristic of the activities of any economic agent, including how a bank reflects uncertainty of its outcome and possible unfavourable consequences (the probability of such events as loss of profits, emergence of losses as a result of non-payment of credits, reduction of the resource base, carrying out payments on off-balance sheet operations), etc.

Some risks are specific to a number of credit institutions or they can constitute systemic banking risks or 'total risks' of all credit institutions. An adverse combination of systemic banking risks when such individual risks are rather high for one bank or a group of banks, and the combination within the entire system may lead to a systemic banking crisis.

External and internal systemic banking risks are differentiated. However, such a division is rather conventional since the systemic banking risks generally tend to include the factors calculated for various risks as well as combined synergies of risks. For example, credit risk (the risk of the counter-agent) is largely connected with the financial standing of the partner, and this condition is defined by currency and market risks, amongst others.

The risks not directly connected with the activity of a bank or its network audience (social groups, legal entities or physical persons who express potential or actual interest in the activity of the bank) belong to the external systemic banking risks. Country risk, currency risk and risk of natural calamities are counted among such risk types.

Country risk is the most difficult to define since it comprises too many factors which are used in its calculation. The country risks increase during a period of globalisation, since banks tend to have more competition from foreign banks. The evaluation of country risk is performed by many famous rating agencies and, in future, must become an important element of the modernised Basel agreements on the assessment of the risks of the banking activities. The country risk first of all comprises the risks of convertibility, transfer and moratorium on payment.

Currency systemic risks comprise commercial, conversion and translational (accounting) risks.

Internal risks depend on the type and peculiarity of banks, the character of their activities and the composition of its counteragents.

The risks of the universal banks, for example, will differ from the risks of the special credit institutes (for example, investment banks or giro central). Universal banks may also have their own specific characteristics, depending upon the type of the clients towards which the bank is oriented. Consequently, such risks are largely defined by the overall structure of the banking system, i.e. and this depends on the relative weight of the total assets and capital of the banking sector; it encompasses both special and universal banks or a form in which the banks service a particular sector or region, etc.

A large group of systemic banking risks comprises those connected with the character of the banking transactions.

There are the risks of passive transactions connected, for example, with excessive dependence on core deposits, i.e. the funds of a few large account owners. These risks could also be expressed in the inability of the credit institutions to ensure adequate lines of credit which, in turn, impacts its potential base of borrowers at the expense of whatever resources it has at its disposal.

In practice, banking regulation and supervision places the main focus on the risks of the active transactions of the banks (credit, portfolio), as well as those risks connected with both the passive and active transactions (the risk of imbalanced liquidity, interest risks).

The systemic credit risk is, probably, the most dangerous to the banking system, more especially in developing and transitional countries. Such a type of risk accumulates in itself and is connected to the influences of other risks (currency, interest). In addition, it is directly dependent upon the macroeconomic situation and the efficiency of the institutional infrastructure (judiciary and taxation systems, credit agency, etc).

In many transitional economies countries that had experienced a series of stock market failures, including those that traded in government securities. Banks were subsequently forced to redirect their orientation to providing credit the kinds of enterprises involved with the so called *real* economy, and this is reflected in how the held shares of such credits in the total credit portfolio of the banks tended to continually increase.

Such a shift in investments is on the one hand, this is the realisation of one of the banks' key functions and, in theory, this should stimulate and encourage normal economic growth. However, under conditions of instable macro-economic situation and inefficiency of judiciary and information institutes there is a tendency of systemic credit risk to be potentially very high. The aggregate systemic risk of the banking sector correspondingly increases, as well as the threat of an impending systemic banking crisis.

Under conditions of globalisation interest and portfolio, systemic risks are becoming rather mobile, since the rate of stocks and other securities today are transnational as never before. Systemic banking crises were largely connected with exactly the same kinds of excessive systemic risks in various countries, take for example, in the United States in 1929, or for the Russian Federation in 1998.

Therefore, the systemic banking crisis exceeds the threshold value of the cumulative systemic risk, which, in turn, is derived from many different inherent banking risks. However, to understand the nature of the systemic crisis, such "division" of derivatives is inadequate, as it does not give a clear picture of the reasons for this phenomenon. Moreover it is necessary to look at the theory of origin of crises, in general, and the banking crises, in particular to understand it better.

1.3. Theories of origins of systemic banking crises

No single interpretation can be provided to describe the concept of a systemic banking crisis and, as with any other kind of macro-economic crisis, can be manifested in various forms, e.g. in the form of a currency or a stock market crisis.

Despite numerous studies in the causes of the Great Depression of the 1930s, there is no consensus towards an encompassing theory. Certainly there is lack of a one-theory-fits-all answer which may be due, in part, to the conflicting views of different economic schools. Nonetheless, because of a definite element of irrationality in the behaviour of various economic agents, and hence, it is impossible to decisively describe or forecast the development or continuation of a crisis. Even so, a number of hypotheses exist to explain economic crises in general, and of problems in the banking sector, in particular, and each can provide specific insight when question are presented as to the actual genesis and progression of given crises.

Nonetheless, many economists studying the nature of systemic banking crises pay special attention to the theory of financial volatility, which describes how the systemic banking risks tend to increase while riding the crest of an economic cycle.

S. Fischer, one of the founders of the quantitative economic theory gives the following interpretation of the economic crisis, in general, and of banking in particular, that:

During economic growth both the investments in the *real* sector of the economy and the intensity of speculations on the financial market tend to grow. The provision of credit plays a significant role in this process. Credit expansion, in its turn, leads to the growth of deposits, money bid and price level. Concurrently the increase of the velocity of money facilitates the growth of credit expansion.

The increase in the price encourages a reduction in the actual values of debts that compensates an increase in the nominal debt. Thus, favourable situations are accompanied by the reduction of the real value of indebtedness which, in turn, triggers further loans. Consequently, so called "excessive" indebtedness emerges in the economy, the level of which becomes critical as a result of the high probability of non-payment of credits and because of insolvency on the part of the lenders.

The crisis originates in the moment when a significant number of the lenders face the problem of a lack of liquidity in not being able to repay current liabilities Creditors of the insolvent borrowers may then demand the sale of the collateral which secured the loan. Massive sell-off of collateral assets as in the case of real estate could then lead to a significant drop in prices throughout the economy (deflationary pressures). Concurrently, because of the growth of systemic credit risks, credit restriction is then implemented by lenders. The resulting curtailment of volume of credit causes brings about a drop in a bank's deposits which affects the rate of the accompanying deflation.

Hence, deflation increases the real value of the debts and makes repayment even more difficult. To meet obligations with increased real value, the borrowers have to sell their assets, including stocks and bonds which, in turn, lead to a subsequent drop in the value of the exchange instruments, and the process causes general deflation. Concurrently, already existing adverse economic conditions further undermine the confidence of creditors and depositors in the banking institutions. As a result, the likelihood of these being a massive withdrawal of deposits becomes even more probable. The possibility of the systemic risk of imbalanced liquidity in the banking sector substantially increases as a result.

Therefore, excessive indebtedness leads to the increase of the systemic credit risk and systemic risk of imbalanced liquidity. If in such a situation the speculative capital "is frightened" and starts to flow out from the economy and banking system of one or another country, to more promising or secure markets; the emergence of the systemic banking crisis is practically unavoidable.

Fischer's theory of crises was further developed in the studies by H. Minsky who defined the financial instability as a correlation of three types of business financing: hedging, speculative and so called "Ponzi financing".

Hedging financing is based on the sufficiency of money resource inflow to repay current payments on the principal and to cover the interest with additional credit.

Speculative financing emerges if there is enough money inflowing only to cover interest repayments, and in order repay the principal new loans are required.

Ponzi financing occurs when there is deficit of the money inflow for the repayment of both the principal and the interest. So, the need for increased borrowings emerges.

H. Minsky assumes that due to the psychological disregard of the possibility of a crisis and strife for profit in the phase of growth, hedging financing is replaced by speculative financing. At a certain moment under the influence of certain exogenous factors (for example, the consequences of the interest rate growth), speculative financing is substituted by Ponzi financing. In such an instance the accumulation of excessive indebtedness and origination of the systemic crisis are inevitable.

The theory of financial instability is further development in the studies of Kindleberger who identified investors and creditors "irrational behaviour' as the main culprit of systemic banking crises because of those who continue investing in overvalued assets in order to obtain large profit margins. The key concepts of his theory include euphoria and panic as demonstrated on the financial markets. To denote the circumstances preceding the crisis, Kindelberger introduced a German term Tourschlusspanic "rush to the gates as it is closing." True, if we take into consideration, the rapid development of the stock market in the United States in the 1990s (especially of the securities of high-tech companies) and not to mention the collapse of this market at the turn of 20th and 21st centuries, and such a crisis theory appears most convincing.

The representatives of the monetarist school (M. Freedman, A. Schwartz) claim that there is no direct dependence between banking crises and the phases of economic cycles. The banking crisis could occur in the absence of an economic recession, and the economic recession is not necessarily accompanied by the crisis in the banking sector. Inadequate level of confidence to the banking institutes by creditors and the population and triggered by the bankruptcy of some large bank or a group of banks could be the cause of financial panic. . The bankruptcy of banks could then negatively affect the economic situation in the country as a whole. According to the monetarists, the Central Bank as "the lender of last resort" can avert the systemic banking crisis by providing the banks with adequate influx of cash.

The supporters of the theory of rational expectations have their own opinions on the origin of currency and banking crises. The basis for this approach is that the investors' behaviour on the financial markets is determined by their rational expectations. Investors build up their policy proceeding from forecasted price on assets. The forecast itself is based on the foundations of mathematical expectations of this value that is conventional in terms of the volume of information known at the time. However, in practice investors' rational expectations could significantly divert from the value due to the fundamental development trends of financial markets. Consequently, due to so called "bubbles" caused by forces of distorted financial markets and their assessment, the threat of a systemic crisis tend to be disguised .

The theory of rational expectations is based on the probable approach to the assessment of the situation but it proves helpless in the face of the uncertainty principle, which in the economic surrounding bears enormous importance.

Globalisation, no doubt, has brought about the growth of various uncertainties, thus motivating many researchers to work on the theory of crises under condition of ever-increasing uncertainty. A number of authors offer to address uncertainty by introducing additional premium for mitigating risks. However, under condition of acute competition in the banking sector, there are rather restricted limitations in being able to establish a premium to cover additional risks.

Theory of credit rationing is founded upon the theory of financial instability and the principle of uncertainty. Adherents of credit rationing theory state that banks provide credits based on the subjective assessment, and the degree of risk is incorporated into the interest rates charged. Such an assessment could be significantly different from the actual level of risk and the experience of the evaluator is important. Furthermore, any evaluator, experience or not, may be suffering from psychological difficulties, thus it is not possible to effectively review the earlier risk assessments, or take all necessary information into consideration. Consequently, when the situation in the economy and the banking sector is relatively calm, the magnitude of risk underassessment is the expansion credit (easy credit), and when faced with any unfavourable external factor, the banks start reviewing their credit portfolios and identify increased credit risk. If this is the case, credit restriction is introduced, thus triggering the bankruptcy of companies that have based their business plans and policies on access to credit lines and widespread bankruptcies of both corporative and banking sectors are most likely.

The Theory of Asymmetric Information has become especially vogue in recent times. This theory was developed in the works by F. Mishkin and Nobel Prize winners J. Stiglitz and J. Akerloff.

The theory connects the occurrence of the financial instability and systemic banking crises with the fact that financial market stakeholders' have unequal access to different levels of information. In practice, asymmetric information leads to the following problems:

Firstly, this is, so called, selection of the worst credit contracts, which is due to the fact that the banks in the status of creditors do not have access to sufficient amounts of information needed to properly assess the credit capacity of a borrower before approving a loan. Consequently, banks are more involved making loans to the kind of borrowers that are less reliable but more active in seeking credit.

Secondly, in case of asymmetry of information, there are instances where the moral risk of a borrower to launch a highly profitable but super-risky activity after obtaining a credit could arise.

The uneven distribution of information and its overall deficit, firstly, for the banks-creditors under certain conditions, as in case of negative external influence, could result in financial instability and a subsequent systemic banking crisis.

In a number of studies by Krugman (1991), Flood and Garber (1988), Miller and Willer (1988), Frut and Obstfield (1992), the eruption of systemic banking crises is connected not with the irrational behaviour of the economic agents, but with some parameters (exchange rate, inflation, money supply) as established by monetary authorities. The profiteers could trigger the crisis in such cases with the expectation that the monetary authorities would respond in terms of a predetermined intervention scenario. Furthermore, the monetary authorities may not have sufficient resources to fend off the attack of speculative capital. Such situation was observed in the countries of South-East Asia, for example, in Malaysia where the government officially blamed the speculative capital, particularly, financial group of G. Soros, for the collapse of the national currency and beginning of a systemic banking crisis.

Take for instance, as reported in a number of studies, by Krugman (1987), the eruption of a currency crisis for instance is explained by so called trigger points. In terms of this theory, the players themselves define a number of points (for example, the position of the exchange rate) for themselves, and if this point is approached, they will carry out predetermined actions, as to react by selling currency). Alternatively, when faced with some unpredicted event, as in the case of some adverse external impact and the market unexpectedly crosses trigger points, the investors' planned vigorous actions could in turn trigger the crisis.

Serious attention in noted in the economic literature to the interconnection of the systemic banking crisis with currency crisis and that of a balance of payment crisis. True, in the majority of the countries so called "double" crisis occurs (combination of a systemic banking crisis and currency crisis). "Double" crisis have been observed in the Scandinavian countries, Turkey, Mexico, Argentine, Venezuela, Bulgaria, countries of South East Asia and Russia.

According to Stoker the crisis of the balance of payment leads to the systemic banking crisis. His study explains how crises exist under conditions where there is an external negative impact and fixed exchange rate results in a significant loss of gold and foreign currency reserves, a growth in the interest rate, credit restriction, the subsequent chain of bankruptcies and an ensuring systemic crisis.

However, F. Mishkin has taken the opposite position to such a professional opinion. He considers that the currency crisis is attributed to the growth of the international interest rates, deterioration of the banking balance sheet and increase in the level of uncertainty on the financial market.

Overall, the majority of researchers note that the systemic banking crisis more often than not preceded a currency crisis. And the economic recession, or at least a 'slow down' of economic growth and deterioration of the key macro-economic indices are precede both kinds of crises. In case of double crises, the key macro-economic indices are significantly worse than prior to a separate currency or banking crisis. Furthermore, double crises tend to be deeper and last longer.

Therefore, that is a lack of any one most appropriate theory that explains the origin of a systemic crisis. However, it is still possible to clearly formulate the factors responsible for such crises.

1.4. Macro-economic and structural causes of systemic banking crises

The banking system permeates through all spheres of modern society, its economy, political life, and social fabric. Consequently any adverse external and internal changes in the social economic organism affect the banking sector and in turn, responsible for causing essential imbalance and a resulting systemic crisis. Such a crisis could erupt as a result of sharp negative impacts of macro-economic factors, as well as a consequence of accumulation of internal imbalances in the banking sector. These negative effects have resulted in the last 20 years in destructive consequences and with financial globalisation, the impacts have became more frequent and intense.

The globalisation of the financial markets occurs along with the deregulation and liberalisation of the flow of international capital across borders, as well as along with the development of the advanced technologies allowing those in the sector to carry out transactions on various financial markets simultaneously. It is manifested not only in the increase of the trans-border mobility of capitals but also in removal of borders between various financial transactions. For example, the banks in addition to their traditional functions of financial dealers are more often involved in performing the function of dealers on the stock exchange and currency markets, both on their own behalf and for the account of various clients.

As a result, the key function of banks – the investment financing leading to the creation of job places and real wealth – is substituted by speculative financial transactions. The change of the behaviour of the credit institution occurs at the background of diluting the borders between various segments of the financial market, for example, between the markets where deals on short-term securities and the markets where deals with long-term loan capital are performed. Speculative banking transactions lead to the excessive increase in their market and the level of interest rates and which impacts systemic banking risks and the various perspectives to the crisis.

The financial globalisation also led to the enhancement of contradiction between the production growth rate of goods and services (so called real economy) and the growth rate of financial transactions (of the financial field). Since 1991, the stock price on the stock exchange of France and Great Britain has doubled, and in the United States - has increased more than three times. It is worth mentioning that the speculative boom on the financial markets in the US and a western country in the 1920s was a contributing factor that encouraged the worldwide depression of the 1930s.

When the banks are too much involved in speculative transactions, it leads, as the practice of the last years demonstrated to the excessive increase in market and interest rates, which brings about systemic banking risks, and from this perspective – contributes to a systemic crisis.

Globalisation is connected with the development of financial derivatives and such an instrument has become independent in terms of its base assets. The scale of such transactions is well demonstrated by the following data: the daily output of the deals on the world currency market increased from USD 1 billion to USD 1.200 billion in the last two decades, while the output of the world trade with goods increased only by 50 percent. The annual value of the world trade in goods and services is equivalent to the five-day value of the operation on the currency markets. Many banks eagerly embraced this financial instrument, since speculative income earning operations with them could bring about unimaginable returns. However, like other speculative operations, there are two sides of the coin in operations involving derivatives. Namely, they suffer from a high degree of volatility and credit risk and too frequently cited as a key factor responsible for the eruption or contribution to full-scaled systemic banking crises.

Aside from the already enumerated global factors, the following causes of the systemic banking crises should also be described:

The extent of the influence of the crisis in the economy on the banking system depends on many factors. The decline of production and deterioration of the solvency of the enterprises-borrowers of the banks are listed as the traditional reasons for a banking crisis. However, it is important to identify the root cause – the pre-existing condition of the banking system itself at the beginning of an accompanying economic crisis. Firstly, there is the liquidity position of banks that is to be considered, which includes the quality of the credit portfolio and adequacy of capital. The presence of systemic imbalances in the banking sector, as a result of undercapitalisation or out of all proportion liquidity is enough for the systemic banking crisis to erupt, and this can materialise even in the absence of significant changes in the economic market conditions.

Excessive credit expansion during the long-term economic upsurge, as a rule, also acts as a factor triggering a banking crisis. The deterioration of the quality of the credit portfolio, over-valuation of the loan collateral and an increase of the systemic credit risk is another side of the credit expansion. This is often concurrent to accelerated growth of the credit which result from its fast change, and this impedes the regulatory authorities in the ability to monitor the quality of the banks' credit portfolios.

In the last two decades, the credit expansion preceded the banking crises in many countries, including Japan, and the countries of Latin America (in the 1980s), and countries of South-East Asia (in the 1990s). For example, on the wave of the 1997 crisis in South Korea, bad and hopeless debts increased from 12.2 trillion to 22.6 trillion Won in absolute terms, and the relative share of the bad and hopeless debts in the credit portfolio increased from 3.9 percent to 6.0 percent.

The liberalisation of the credit markets in Sweden entailed the boom of the 1980s which was accompanied by speculative borrowing and inflation in the financial market then followed, resulting in a serious crisis. Experts consider that the costs of the banking recapitalisation in 1991 comprised 6.4 percent of the GDP. Overnight in 1992, the interest rates jumped to 500 percent, i.e., and the government failed to stop further devaluation even when buttressed with fiscal policy (attempts attaching the Krona to Ecu in anticipation of Sweden's accession into European Union, which subsequently proved unsuccessful).

Other than high economic growth rates in South-East Asia, the vulnerability of the banking system has been concealed for many years. The continued demand for the credits was persistent until the economy was able to grow. Nonetheless, the most recent crisis uncovered poor quality of the credit portfolios of many banks. Fault could be attributed to both government and the Central Bank, and this was in part because they prevented the changes in the value of local currencies in the beginning, while there was a large inflow of the foreign capital, and later, in the presence of dramatic outflows, governments of these countries would actually encourage excessive credits to various enterprises. For example, in Thailand excessive credit expansion was noticeable in the real estate sector. In Malaysia direct borrowing occurred in various sectors, and especially among small businesses.

In South Korea the government was tolerant towards different types of financial companies which were vigorously set up. The number of banking transactions was carried out to avoid stricter regulations being applied to the banks and 'Chebol' – large financial-industrial groups that is of a clan nature. The government turned a blind eye and silently approved some of their fallacious activities as obtaining linked loans. The experience of these countries indicates that the credit growth more than twice exceeding the GDP growth, which is a sign of a pending banking crisis.

Inflation remains as one of the key macro-economic factors for the eruption of a systemic banking crisis. The banking sector is affected through several channels – via interest rates, weakening of stimuli for savings and a reduction of the deposit base; outflow of national capitals abroad, change of the structure of active (aggressive, dynamic) and passive banking operations.

During periods of inflation the assets and profits could grow at a fast rate but as a rule in nominal terms. Concurrently, those financial institutes whose assets have longer term of allocation than the terms for claiming liabilities are presented a difficult situation. Depositors, especially under conditions of high price growth have the option of responding to the reduction of the real interest rates negatively that are poised by the banks; primarily if there are alternative options for investing savings.

In the period of high growth rate of prices in most of the countries banks tend to significantly reduce the terms for the credit contracts, and target borrowers who demonstrate high rates of capital turnover. Since one of the fundamental functions of the banks is transformation of current savings into long-term investments, any dramatic reduction of the terms of the contracts with unavoidable reduction of investment financing could be perceived as the "washing out" of financial institutes. Reduction in the terms of credit contracts significantly undermines the stability of the banks and makes them more vulnerable to market fluctuations.

Some banks are unable to increase the nominal interest rates to the level that would ensure positive real interest on deposits when exposed to a period of inflation. The result is the outflow of deposits from the banks and transformation of investments into other kinds of financial assets. Amongst countries with ramified system of financial institutes and developed financial markets, the funds released from the banks would still be allocated on the national markets. For example, on the wave of inflation, mutual funds tended to be set up that enticed the depositors from the banks and other deposit pools. Where the capacity of alternative deposits is restricted or limited,, the outflow of the national capital from the country becomes that much more active, as was the case in transitional economies under conditions of financial liberalisation.

Sharp price fluctuations in the cost of goods, financial assets, and interest rates significantly increase under conditions of general economic uncertainty and system risks in relations of banks with their main counterparts – depositors, borrowers and regulatory authorities. The evaluation of credit and market risks by banks is a rather complicated process, and depositors and regulatory authorities find it difficult to ascertain the financial condition and health of banks. The comparison of the countries that have experienced banking crisis with the countries where no crisis was found, demonstrates that in the former case, the index variation co-efficient of the consumer prices is more than three times higher than in the former case.

Factors demonstrating a character of external economic nature play an important role in the origination of systemic banking crises, was demonstrated in the early 1980s. Such crises, as experienced in many developing countries, are frequently associated with an accompanying drop in oil prices on international markets and a decrease in the value in other key export commodities

Another significant factor, an increase of foreign debt servicing costs, which is also a factor a in explaining the dramatic increase in interest rates among lenders in western countries. A dramatic growth of the foreign debt in developing countries comes at a price, and is contingent to the added expense of increased, having to seek funding at the international level, which often precedes corresponding crises.

As a result, and upon the evaluation of the value of the market refinancing and accompany devaluation of the national currencies, which results in the accompany insolvency of the banks, and provides yet another contributing factor to a foreign debt crisis. The depth of a crisis and how long-lasting it continues is due in part that many governments have attempted, with mixed results, exercise, and inflationary, monetary and fiscal policy in an inadequate policy environment. Sound policy process mechanisms systems are essential in assuring appropriate and effective banking oversight.

It was characteristic, in the 1990s, the re-occurrence of systemic banking crises in many developing countries. However, the scale and intensity was even larger to be expected, and despite all the measures taken to augment banking supervision and the significant improvement made in the spheres of macro-economic policy and even when implemented a timely fashion. Many programs were carried out with the direct participation and control of international financial institutions (IFI-s), such as the IMF and the World Bank.

Currency and financial shocks in the form of substantial devaluation of the national currency and a spike of interest rates interrupted the period of rapid economic growth, and this progression was accompanied by a speculative boom in the stock exchange and real estate market. Many problems resulted, including the insolvency of the many credit institutions. There was also a concurrent loss of public confidence in the economy standing of various countries and regions, especially among those investors involved with international portfolio, and when combined with the activities of large currency speculators, a resulting eruption and diffusion of the systemic banking crises, occurred.

Notwithstanding such processes, a marked deterioration in the conditions of foreign trade in the majority of the countries where banking crises had occurred was obvious. According to information provided by the World Bank on 29 countries experiencing systemic banking crisis, the conditions for trade tended to deteriorate a few years earlier than the actual crisis each experienced. Overall the pre-crisis decline in the volume of the foreign trade reached a level of 17 percent. The indicator for those countries that had partial crises comprises 4 percent of the total, whereas among those countries where systemic crises were noticed, overall trade conditions improved.

The policy of the fixed national currency rate applied in order to stabilise the prices in some countries brought about depletion of the foreign currency reserves of the Central Banks which is clearly demonstrated with the example of the banking crisis in Russia in 1998.

Therefore, considering the above, a systemic banking crisis is the result of the influence of multiple of macro-economic and structural factors, least being, the impact of institutional factors and their overall role on the banking sector.

1.5. Institutional factors of systemic banking crises

Institutional factors are of a significant importance when dealing with issue describing the genesis and progressing of systemic banking crises.

Social institutes also have a direct influence on economic development, though, according to the representatives of many economic schools, for example, institutionalists (Veber, Veblen, Gelbreit), this influence is an important factor, both for economic growth and its relation to banking crises.

However, it largely depends on the institutional infrastructure, as the banking sector is contingent upon the highest level of technology, including IT, and is the most risky (accumulates the risks of almost all fields, regions and countries) within its sphere. It is paramount to highlight the importance of the quality of the regulation and banking supervision.

The banking regulation and supervision of the 1970s and 1980s seriously lagged behind the rate of rapidly increasing risks associated with banking activities. Based upon the findings of a World Bank survey in 29 countries, having experienced systemic banking crisis, shortcomings in supervision and regulation were identified as being the main responsible factors for the crises. The crises in many developed countries including the crisis in Savings and Loans Associations in the United States are also first explained by the problems in this field. In the developing countries in the 1980s, the relation of the capital with the weighted by risks assets comprised less than 5 percent being obviously insufficient. In many countries the definition of the outstanding credits was rather light. For example, in Malaysia till 1990 the credits not provided for more than a year were considered as being outstanding. In many Latin America the fiscal reserve requirements assuring repayment of losses were actually underestimated.

The epidemics of banking crises in the 1980s certainly pushed the reforms in the spheres of regulation and supervision forward, and banking regulation in the last 15 years has undergone dramatic changes, and the leading role for spearheading these reforms belongs to the Basel Committee for Banking Regulation and Supervision.

The Basel agreement of 1988 addresses the method of capital valuation and the degree of the assets risk, and is thought as a logical response by banking authorities in this sphere who were located in the industrially developed countries to react to the new threats most associated with the growth of financial instability. The concerted response was based upon approved methodology taking into consideration various types of risks (country risk, risk of the counteragent, credit risk), etc, while at the same time calculating the capital adequacy ratio. Concurrently, the changes in supervision and regulation on the international level apparently lagged behind the destructive changes being faced on the global level.

However, the Agreement of 1988 did not take into consideration interest and market risks. These had to be accounted for in the face of the high volatility of the assets value, including securities, in the first place, which as these were thought not to be that frequently as factor triggering a systemic banking crisis. Moreover, such agreements also did not consider the risks connected with operations existing off the balance sheet, including derivatives markets, while these operations and risks were rapidly increasing. Therefore, agreement of 1988 could not be called an adequate response to the challenges faced at the time. Nonetheless, it proved an important step forward.

Transitional countries having entered the path of the market reforms in the late1980s and into the early 1990s in the absence of adequate banking regulations were unable to keep up with necessary institutional changes in compliance with social and economic changes. Furthermore, obvious weaknesses in governmental institutes were observed, and which accompanied inefficient legal framework in the field of supervision. It is rather certain that these played a significant role in the emergence of systemic banking crises, not only in these specific countries but elsewhere as well.

In the 1990s, the Basel agreement experienced further changes, and currently, methods of determining interest, market risks, and other risks connected with the off-balance sheet operations as used in many countries. New agreements came into effect in 2005. They gave the banks substantial possibilities of setting up effective systems of risk management on the basis of their own methods of applying the information of rating agencies, for example, 'Value-At-Risk.' However, the quality of the regulation and supervision in the various developed and transitional economies failed to meet the objectives of early problem diagnosis in the banking sector and to have taken the necessary steps for timely and effective prevention.

The majority of the researchers focusing on systemic banking crises name the absence or inefficiency of the deposit insurance system as being another important institutional factor of bringing about crises. Massive withdrawal of deposits from the banks not only deepens the banking crisis but can actually provoke it. As a result, especially in recent years, systems of deposit insurance have since emerged in the majority of developing countries. However, an inefficient deposit insurance system, one that lacks relevant power, adequate financial base, and support from the government, is still not prepared to be a preventing factor that can prevent systemic banking crisis. Such a scenario is well demonstrated when examples of Latin America countries is provided. Thus, a deposit insurance system tends to acquire an obligatory character, and clients funds are secured as a result of governmental involvement, as provided for in the European Union directive of 1994 which stipulated the exact principles of constructing a deposit insurance system.

In addition, an inefficient functioning of the judiciary system can also be a trigger to the eruption and acute progress of systemic banking crises, especially in the absence of an effective mechanism of protection for creditors, and to assure that the rights of investors are such that if prevailing conditions fail to stimulate investments into the authorised capital of the credit institution, giving rise to the temptation for the borrowers to default payback and, thus, there will not be the prevailing conditions for an actual expansion of systemic credit risks. The duration, and sometime quite draw out, and complexity of trials in many countries also acts as a barrier to the effective implementation of supervisory authorities and their authority, and impends the effect implementation of a deposit insurance systems. Such problems have been noted in terms of the cancellation or revoking of the licences for the banks, whose activities threaten the creditors' interests and such action could contribute to wider instances of non-repayment and an excess of bad debts in the banking sector.

Alongside the judiciary system, an unreasonable tax system also impacts the otherwise stable functioning of the banking sector. Absence of the tax concessions, for example, on investments in the banking capital, or in terms of the provision of long-term credits does not encourage sustainable development of the banking system.

Information asymmetry is the theory that attributes the genesis of the systemic crises to the absence of the relevant institutes which could otherwise provide the banking sector with the information on the potential borrowers. According to another World Bank survey, experts in the countries that went through the systemic banking crisis, note fraud as a factor driving such crises and this is listed on the eighth place, and overtakes such factors as the concerted withdrawal of the deposits and other shortcomings inherent the judiciary system. Among most transitional countries, credit bureaus or the centres analysing the economic condition of markets in various fields of economy and regions do not actually exist. Meanwhile, in the majority of the developed countries such institutes emerged many decades ago, and they have been transformed to new levels of qualitative oversight and are now development.

The development of mortgage lending could be an alternative to working with banking assets hat that are high volatile (potential being a threat leading to a systemic banking crises). However, in the majority of transitional countries the relevant institutional infrastructure (special government mortgage agencies, legislation covering mortgage securities) either does not exist or are not that developed.

Such institutes as specialised banks, or agencies for the development of this or that fields, regions, export-import operations, settlement and payment systems do not exit, and their absence in many countries significantly lowers the potential of the banking sector and makes the financial institutions vulnerable to the banking crisis.

CHAPTER 2
Banking system restructuring as a comprehensive plan of action for overcoming crisis and creating sustainable and dynamic banking sector

2.1. Restructuring as a plan of action for overcoming systemic banking crises

Searching out ways to overcome systemic crises and create a sustainable and dynamic banking sector has been enjoyed on the highest priority. This has been the case on both the national and international level.

Important steps have been taken on the international level in recent years. Much is related to the activities of the Basel committee in forming a new banking regulatory and supervisory system, and one that is more adequate to the nature and the degree of the risks of the banking activities under the conditions of global financial instability. Such attempts are being vigorous followed and new concepts are now in place that deals with reforming of the International Monetary Fund and other international financial organisations. The purpose is to increase the efficiency of their activities, and especially when faced with regional epidemics within the systemic banking. Solutions for banking crises are actively being sought after. New deposit insurance systems are either being created or reformed worldwide. The objective is to effectively stabilise banking systems. There is a significant association between the existence of a deposit insurance system and problem resolution.

Many countries have restructured their banking systems on the national level, which has included the implementation of strategic measures designed to overcome the acute phase of the crisis and the subsequent elaboration of long-term strategies necessary for the continued development of the banking system.

The term "restructuring" translated from Latin means change, improvement of the structure of some object or system. Restructuring implies not only removal of the destructive and outdated phenomena but also transition of an object or a system to a qualitatively new level, essential improvement of their adaptation to the changed external conditions.

In the economics the term "restructuring" is often used in the following word combinations: debt restructuring, including external indebtedness; restructuring of payment and (trade) balance of payment; restructuring of the corporate sector of economy and particular enterprises; restructuring of the banking sector.

The term "restructuring of the banking sector" came into used relatively recent – approximately since the late 1980s. The governments of many countries, with the participation of international financial organisations started to develop complex anti-crisis programs called "restructuring of the banking sector (system)" as a response to the destructive systemic banking crises they experienced.

In addition, this term has taken on a legal definition in the legislation of many countries, though it strongly varies, depending on the peculiarities of the national legal system. It is generally used to describe "a programme of measures applied to credit institutions and aimed at overcoming a lack of financial sustainability and being able to restore solvency, or alternatively, implementing the liquidation of credit institutions and this to be carried out in compliance with national legislation".

It should be considered that the legal meaning is rather narrowly defined and fails in providing a complete picture of such a multifaceted phenomenon. A complex definition of restructuring of the banking system is as follows: "Under the restructuring of the banking system is understood a process of structural changes in the banking system managed by governments with clear coordination of the activities of all the branches of the power, supported by the relevant amendments in the monetary, tax, budgetary, and information policies of the government, and which is aimed at the formation of reliable systems of universal, regional and specialised banks, dynamically developing and adequately responding to the needs of the national economy".

It is true that the process of structural changes in any given banking system may occur spontaneously. However, the process itself could also be managed by the government. In the former case, the banking institutes are transformed under the influence of some political, economic, legal, moral or even external technological factors.

For example, changes in the money circulation had enormous impact on the structure of the banking system. Firstly comes the emergence of bills and then evolves banknotes, the development of the system of electronic settlement, and continuing on its part of evolution, to the final integration of the banking business with the Internet. This final stage has brought about revolutionary implications on the overall structure of the banking systems.

To further illustrate, the formation of protestant work ethics which consider that the success in business as being one of the most important values, has been an enormous motivater and stimulus on the establishment and formation of what is today the modern banking systems in many countries of Northern and Western Europe.

Alongside of the spontaneous process of the banking system restructuring, the structure formation role of the government is a prominent factor. As the historical experience demonstrates, the level of governmental participation in the restructuring of the banking system varies considerably and is not constant over time and between different countries.

In the majority of the developed countries, the banking systems developed as a result of the development of the bourgeois relations relatively not that long ago – in the 19th century. The government either was involved in establishing or changing the role of the Central Bank, providing for specialised banks, and changing the regulatory and supervisory rules, which included elements of the money system. This is illustrated by introducing or cancelling the adherence to the Gold Standard, which subsequently had a great impact on the structure and operation of the banking system.

For example, establishment of the Bank of France in 1800 or formation of the Federal Reserve System in the United States in 1913 essentially changed the structure of these two banking regulatory systems.

The next stage of the banking systems restructuring is connected with the Great Depression of 1929-1933 that was experienced worldwide. The US became the pioneer in the restructuring of its banking system with the creation of the system of guaranteeing deposits and the provision of a special institute for the overall management of this system. The US simultaneously restructured its problematic credit institutions - Federal Corporation of Deposits Insurance.

A new stage of restructuring of the banking systems is buttressed with a series of events in the banking crises as both developed and developing countries face during periods of financial globalisation and deregulation. The depth and scale of the systemic banking crises continued to build up for the last two decades, affecting whole regions of the world and impacting the world economy as a whole.

For example, 1300 banks and 1400 Saving and Loan associations ceased functioning in the period of 1980 to 1991 in the US. The costs of the restructuring of the banking system according to various appraisals were from USD 200 to 500 billion (5 percent of the total GDP). During the large scale restructuring the banking system of the US, like in many other countries, experienced substantial changes. The result brought about a qualitatively measured new stage of development. Overall, 70 countries were affected by the crises, and for some, the systemic crises proved to be of a repetitive nature. However, in spite of the widespread crisis, a number of countries, such as Great Britain, Netherlands, Denmark, Austria, Switzerland, etc., were able to avert the systemic banking crises, which was largely attributed to the system in place for prevention. The problem of heading off such problems was often because an efficient system of system of banking supervision and regulation was lacking in the first place.

Restructuring of the banking systems on the modern stage can be described as a set of measures starting from the timely diagnosis of the problems existing in credit institutions and the provision of financial assistance to them, and when deemed necessary, the efficient liquidation of various banks by bankruptcy proceedings; and, under such terms and conditions that is often one sided, and the interests of creditors is held to a minimum.

In this chapter we will review virtually the range of existing stages of banking restructuring. With this in mind, an important element of restructuring of the banking system is monetary policy of the Central Bank and the Government.

Central Banks could provide certain forms of assistance to problem banks during a crisis, especially if they are faced with current liquidity problem. For example, in Venezuela eight banks considered solvent used such special lines of liquidity to access financial resources.

In other instances, the provision of credit is a regular step on the part of Central Banks to support stability in the banking system during the financial crisis and thus, to provide the credit institutions the necessary time and resources to carryout restructuring. The National Bank of Poland, which offered a long-term assistance to the restructuring credit institutions, is a good example. The National Bank of Poland purchased low yield stocks and long-term bonds of the banks.

A reduction in the level of the mandatory reserves (or increase of interest payments on them) – is an additional type of assistance rendered by various monetary authorities.

Brazil, for example, released part of its obligatory call deposit reserves to finance the purchase of certificates of time deposits issued by the institutes within their banking restructuring program.

Establishment of the control over the problem banks and their recapitalisation by the government is an important element of the banking system restructuring. As a rule, if a credit institution faces serious problems, supervisory authorities introduce temporary administrative staffing into such banks and they are tasked with preventing further deterioration of the situation, thus averting creditors' panic, and in turn they taking various measures to restrain the crisis and keeping it from spreading to other institutes via the mechanism of inter-bank settlements.

Setting up special institutes is an important part of the banking system restructuring program These are the institutes responsible for the effective restructuring. Generally they are granted significant authority and they carry out their activities in a special legal status that continues for the length of time needed for restructuring.

For example, to recover the banking system in Indonesia, Indonesian Agency for bank restructuring was established and under its conditions authorities made decisions in terms of capitalisation, mergers and liquidation of problem banks. To overcome the last systemic crisis in Indonesia, 54 development banks of the country of which 39 were private, 4 state and 11 regional were passed to this Agency for management.

The next logical step in the restructuring process comes after establishing control over the problem banks and assuring temporary capitalisation for their reorganisation. The key instrument in this process is a merger of a problem bank with financially sound institute or search for a foreign investor willing to purchase the credit institute. Frequently the merger is preceded by clearing of the portfolio of the bank under a reorganisation program from the load of bad credits. If the banks assets turned out to be non-liquid, only its branches and property would then be sold off.

The sale of assets is a rather complicated and long draw out process and requires a special agency. Thus, while restructuring the banking systems, along with the restructuring agencies, the institutes for assets management, securitization and liquidation of problematic credit institutions are also established.

In spite of all these efforts and a bank cannot be rescued, the next choice is for the problem bank to be subjected to liquidation.

A set of operational procedures for revoking licences of credit institutions is another important direction in the restructuring of the banking systems. Such operations addressing the implementation of banking operations come into play when financial problems are severe enough to possibly trigger systemic banking crisis and in the case of borrowing on the inter-bank market and when financial assistance on the part of the government is not expedient or impossible. The experience of a number of countries (Thailand, Malaysia, Latvia, and Russia) demonstrates that artificial prolongation of the existence of instable credit institutions, or those which are difficult to regulate tends to enhance the potential problems and financial losses in the future.

A serious attention is paid to building up transparent and effective liquidation procedures in the majority of countries. This is paramount since the protection of the creditors' interests and financial capabilities of the deposit insurers directly depend on the adequate organisation of this process.

Take for instance the maximum success demonstrated in the sales, use of technologies, reorganisation and the eventual liquidation in the case of problem banks in the US. The activities of the Federal Deposit Insurance Corporation and Trust Corporation made it possible to recover part of the 500 USD billion spent on overcoming the crisis of the Savings and Loans Banks.

Effective banking regulation and supervision are among the key elements in overcoming the systemic banking crisis and creating a sound banking sector. Under conditions of banking system restructuring regulatory and supervisory rules are used the short-term period to mitigate problems.

However, any special regime of regulation and supervision for the period of the crisis is usually offset by formation in the long run of the regulatory and supervisory systems. It is necessary to take the risks of banking activities into closer account. The Basel Committee has recently recommended the national authorities of banking supervision the compound the system of regulating coefficients with the methods of stress testing of the credit institutions and to introduce an adequate system of risk assessment into the banks that proceed from the specificity of their activity. The assessment of business planning in the credit institution is also a very essential factor to consider Sphere of restructuring is a very important one and hence a entire chapter in this book is solely dedicated to this issue.

The recent trends in the world experience of the banking system restructuring demonstrate that more and more responsibility for the unsatisfactory financial status of the banks both in the legal and economic aspects is laid on the owners of the credit institutions and affiliated persons. It is for this reason that the actions of the government to rescue banks by restructuring are faced with difficulties, as in some instances the expectation of assistance could result in reduction in the sense of responsibility on the part of the banking institute over its own activities. Thus, it is extremely important that the condition of any assistance is not provided in such as to where way to encourages irresponsible behaviour in the future.

For example, in South Korea the banks had been asked to partially write off the capital as a condition for assistance. Mexico was taking on bad loans from credit institutions with the conditionality that the shareholders increase the level of authorised capital. In Brazil and India, if the credit institutions went bankrupt, the shareholders had double commitments, i.e. they had to invest equity capital equal to their initial share in the authorised capital fund.

However, shareholders are not the one that always bears the responsibility. For example, if the losses are due to the loans that had been granted at the insistence of the government, the shareholders are not held responsible; this is especially vital for those banking systems with a larger share of governmental participation. It is also important to rate the degree of responsibility, since the shareholders could experience difficulties in detecting problems in the credit institutions because of a lack of transparency and other reporting entanglements, and especially at the early stage of emergence of financial hardships. It can be assumed that the resolution of this problem in the countries with transitional economies is largely connected with the introduction of the International Banking, Accounting and Reporting Standards, as well as an increase in the quality of work and the degree of responsibility accepted by audit companies.

In the 1980s and 1990s, along with other measures of restructuring of the banking system, a deposit insurance system was introduced in many developed and developing countries. This measure has the tendency to secure long-term stability of financial systems. However, it is important to note that the positive impact of the deposit insurance system on the status of the banking sector is only possible only under conditions where supervision is efficient and a deliberate monetary policy is maintained. Otherwise, as it was obvious in looking at the examples of Argentina, Uruguay, Brazil and a few other countries, the deposit guarantee system becomes inefficient and the country needs to find another way to bring about restructuring of its banking system.

To resolve the problem of "informational asymmetry" by means of creation of an institute of "credit bureaus" - especially in the long-term perspective, is also an important element to consider in the restructuring of banking systems.

Governments and central banks have used various schemes in bringing about banking system restructuring. Practice has demonstrated that there is no unique strategy in achieving the improvement of the situation within the banking sector, and in many cases, the implementation of various actions and interventions depends largely on concrete conditions.

However, general integral components of the successful programmes of restructuring implemented by foreign countries can be identified:

- To determine, as soon as possible, the degree of the

existing problem, to recognise it on the national level and to communicate to the authorities the need to allocate substantial financial resources to bring about its solution;

- To use all leverages of influence on the banking sector that the state has to overcome the crisis, including monetary and credit policies, supervision and regulation, re-capitalisation, and the purchase of the problem assets;
- To amend the general, and in particular banking legislation, for the maximum protection of the interests of creditors and investors, by increasing supervisory effectiveness, and to speed up the liquidation of problem banks;
- To create special institutions, such as agencies for restructuring and liquidation, companies to manage assets and ensure their security, deposit insurance systems, and to establish credit bureaux;
- To create comprehensive, transparent and effective restructuring programs.

As the international experience demonstrates, maximum progress in restructuring of the banking system is achieved by creation of specialised institutes. The programme of restructuring of the banking system bears complex, transparent and speedy character.

2.2. Role of monetary and credit policy in averting and overcoming systemic banking crises

Monetary policy joined with the budgetary, structural and tax policies are key state instruments in bringing about economic regulation and ensuring stable growth. The decision to use one or another monetary instrument, allows the government to impact the volume and structure of the money supply, inflation rate, and to smoothen over the consequences of an adverse economic situation. As the experience of the last two decades has thoroughly demonstrated, the application of monetary policy is essential for successful restructuring of banking systems to come about.

A dual role is played out by the banking system in connection with the monetary policy: on the one hand, the banking system is a transmitting link of monetary policy, and on the other, liquidity and financial stability of the credit institution often act as one of the goals and objectives of such a policy.

Certain elements of the monetary policy on the part of the government comes in the form of governmental and inter-governmental credits, issuance and purchase of the government securities, currency interventions, and regulation of the interest rates on credits, as has been observed over various historical periods. For example, legislative restrictions on interest rates on credits could be found in the ordinances of French King Henry IV (16th century). Government credits and operations with government securities of the monetary authorities became a usual practice in England and France already in the 18th and 19th centuries.

However, monetary and credit policy in modern sense calls for at least three elements:

1. Flexible money supply comprising not only cash but bank deposits as well;
2. Developed credit institutions carrying out non-cash settlements, transactions with currency, bills, government and corporate securities;
3. A single issuing and regulating body called a Central, National or State Bank.

Such conditions were established in 18-19th centuries in the majority of developed countries, and since then, such monetary instruments as account policy of the Central Bank, operations on the open market with securities and currency, and these have been widely applied in achieving regulation objectives.

Account policy or the policy of refinancing of commercial banks has always played an essential part in the monetary policy of the state. Already in 19th century, central banks of the developed countries by amending a rate regulated the bank liquidity and eventually affected the economic situation in the country. Since the account policy only brings about a virtual determination of the value of money and it is deprived of administrative influence elements and this is unlike the liabilities of the reserve requirements. The effectiveness of this instrument depends largely on the level of the development of monetary and credit relations within the country. In those countries with high level of monetisation of the economy and that have developed banking system, and change of the Central Bank rate by several percentage points brings about large-scale economic impacts. However, on the whole, still does not lead to significant fluctuations. For example, the rate of the European Central Bank in 1999-2002 despite the changing macro-economic parameters and tactical goals of the monetary authorities, varied within 3.00 – 4.95 percent.

However, because of an inadequate level in the development of the monetary relations in transitional economies, such a monetary credit policy instrument is of a rather formal nature and is predominately used for tax settlement, fine imposition, etc.

Early in the 20th century, monetary and credit policy became part of the central bank tools – in maintaining required reserve requirements. The studies of the economists of the neo-classical school (Marshal, Pigu, and Patinkin) in the field of structure of the money supply and banking multiplier proved to be the theoretical foundation that was used in justifying the existence of minimal reserve requirements among commercial banks. It was Marshal who provided the following assessment of the dependence of the banking multiplier and obligatory reserves, "...we have geometric progression, and if each individual bank were able to accommodate two thirds of its deposits, the total size of the credit facilities of these banks would be three times higher than if there was a different situation. If the banks were able to accommodate four fifths of their deposits, their credit facilities would be five times higher, etc. The question of what part of its deposits the bank could accommodate largely depends on the size of the direct or indirect reserves generated by the bank".

Today minimal reserve requirements serve two main functions:

Firstly, they represent a mechanism of liquidity regulation of any particular bank and provide for the overall liquidity of the banking system. Changing the norm of the obligatory reserves, depending on the economic situation, the Central Bank supports the extent of the liquidity of a commercial bank and the banking system as a whole; these mechanisms are used to maintain a feasible minimum liquidity level.

Secondly, minimum reserve requirements provide an instrument for regulating the volume of the money supply in circulation within the country by alternating the size of credit-deposit reserve.

These two functions are of macro-economic importance, and if significance of the second function larger scale is certainly assured from its content, then in turn the macro-economic significance of the first function is based on how an adequate liquidity level is able to heads off systemic banking risks.

Furthermore, macro-economic content of the minimal reserve requirements supports the function and role of the banking system within the economy, and especially for commercial banks as a whole. Such determinants provide the key channel for supplying the economy with financial resources and determining the buying power of the currency. R. Goldsmith coefficient reflecting the relationship of the financial sector and real wealth, as demonstrated for 20 years (from the 1970s to 1990s) increased value in the developed countries more than to 30 percent, of which in Great Britain – to 90 percent and in the US – to 40 percent. Such sustained growth under conditions of exercising monetary policy reinforces the ever-increasing influence of the banking system on the overall macroeconomic situation.

The Federal Reserve System of the US was the first to apply the minimum reserve requirements.

Prior to 1930s, the level of the obligatory reserves of the banks-members of FRS did not alter, nor was it revised. In 1933, the Federal Reserve System was authorised to vary the set requirements for reserves. Initially the FRS was granted the right to change the level of the reserves but no more than twice the level of the existing one, and even when this was done, each decision had to be approved by the American President.

Such permission was only granted under emergency or conditions of urgency. In 1935 the Law *On Banks and Banking Activities* that legalised this procedure as a standard operational instrument for the banking business and then presidential control over this issue was cancelled. Within the range of established maximum and minimum levels, authorities of the FRS maintained the right to amend the reserve levels, and could either adjust them in an upward or downward direction.

This was a time in American banking history that the banking sphere had significant excess reserves volume as a result of an acute banking crisis. In the period, 1936-1937, tightening the requirements toward the level of the required reserves was implemented for the first time. This was the starting point and now the control by the FRS over the reserve levels was being fully carried out, The FRS started fixing the reserves among member-banks. The Board of Directors of FRS, and as approved by the Congress and responsibilities revised on an as needed basis, was responsible for controlling these levels.

Moreover, the attitude of the FRS towards cash balances, which is considered as banking reserves, changed several times during the period of its functioning. The initial law on FRS (1913) allowed the member-banks of the FRS to consider half of the cash balance in their possession in addition to their reserve deposits in the Federal Reserve Banks as being their own reserves. Later, from 1917 to 1959, only the deposits in the Federal Reserve Banks were qualified as reserves, and starting from 1960, member-banks of FRS were allowed to count all their cash balance as reserve funds.

In 1970, the level of required reserves comprised for time the deposits from 3 to 10 percent and deposits on demand from 10 to 25 percent, and as such, banks acting as reserve cities, and maintained from 7 to 14 percent in terms of the banks of regional banks. Later, beginning from the same period, the level of required reserves gradually decreased.

After publishing the Law *On Control over the Money Circulation* (1980), there was a reduction in the number of deposits where obligatory reserve repayment was introduced. In addition, unified requirements to the reserves were established and these were obligatory for all types of deposit organisations; the differentiation of the level for minimum reserves was revoked, and depending on the reserving rank of the banks, a new classification of deposit accounts of credit institutions was introduced. Moreover, the requirements toward private (individual) deposits and time deposits were cancelled. The same law reduced the obligatory norm of the reserve repayment from 5 percent to 2 percent. The FRS retained the right to amend the level of the obligatory reserves.

The new legislation envisaged that as a result of such transformations, the FRS would now actively apply this instrument of control over monetary and credit relations. However, the opposite of expectations actually transpired. Since 1980, the FRS has since revised its own requirements as to the level of reserves, albeit, very rarely, and such alternations have been carried out rather cautiously. Hence the FRS strives to implement its policy in fighting both deflation and inflation processes, as they continue to emerge. FRS bears responsibility for the application of the instruments of its policy to avert the national crisis of liquidity and financial panic in a critical situation in its statutory role as the creditor of last resort. Presently the norms of the obligatory reserves are established by means of so called "D" regulations as provided by the FRS's Board of Directors.

In the post World War II period, this instrument of monetary and credit policy has been applied in the majority of developed countries.

The German Bundesbank is authorised to set the level of required reserves in terms of current commitments not being higher than 30 percent, on time deposits –no more than 20 percent, and for \savings deposits – not to exceed 10 percent. Within such limits the Central Bank of Germany could vary the levels depending on the regulatory objectives. . In compensation for the need for the Central Bank to maintain interest-free reserves, commercial banks enjoy a number of allowances: non-cash settlement turnover via Bundesbank is free; adding up the excessive funds available in the commercial banks to meet the commitments of minimal reserves; minimal reserves could serve as working assets.

In some instances, the reserve obligations could be accomplished by the purchase of government securities with a particular purpose in mind – to finance the state budget. However, checks were in place, and if the banks fail to meet the reserve requirements, Bundesbank would imposes a fine on the banks in the form of a special interest during a period of 30 days. As a rule, the special interest exceeds the interest rate on collateral loan extended by German Federal Bank to the credit institutions by a margin of 3 percent.

One of the methods of the monetary and credit regulation of the French economy on the part of the Central Bank is change of the level of obligatory reserves maintained for credit institutions.
Presently the Board of the Bank of France determines monetary and credit policy, the calculation base and sets the levels of obligatory reserves in compliance with the law of 1993 "On the Charter of the Bank of France, its Activities and Supervision over the Credit institutions."

Required reserves are kept in the Bank of France in an interest-free account. The reserve requirements are like what was introduced in 1967 in the US, and is fixed at the level of 4.5 percent on checks and current accounts, and 2 percent on other types of liabilities. In the period from 1967 to 1983, the Bank of France amended the reserve standards several times. In the later 1980s, the required reserves for time and savings deposits increased from 0.75 percent to 1 percent for demand deposits – increasing from 4.2 percent to 5 percent. Such a difference was largely connected with the cancellation of the quantitative credit restrictions in the country as of January 1987. It is because of violation of the levels of required reserves, the credit institutions were obligated to pay fine and these as a rule exceeds the rate by 3 percent.

Overall, the size of the norm of reserves seriously varies from country-to-country, and it depends on the inflation rate, the condition of the economic cycle and the financial status of banks. In Great Britain this indicator comprises 0.45 percent, in Japan – from 0.125 to 2.5 percent, in Switzerland – 2.5 percent, in Germany – from 4.15 to 12.1 percent, in France – from 3 to 5.5 percent and in Spain – 17 percent.

Although today this monetary instrument is recognised by the majority of experts as an economic facility that is most effective. However, caution must be used. Many economists, especially bankers-practitioners, often even call for cancellation of this instrument of monetary and credit policy, since it draws down a significant portion of resources and out of the bank's circulation. The diversion of these resources leads to the valuation of the liabilities which in turn forces the banks to compensate these costs, and either by increasing income from active transactions (high income is always connected with a higher risk), or by means of reducing various costs within the bank.

We can assume that the reserve requirements are able to contribute to a positive role in maintaining the liquidity of the banking system, and this is brought about by a so called "enforced measure" – which is essential when faced with the threat of a pending banking crisis. The mechanism of functioning of this instrument calls for corrections as needed. For example, to improve the liquidity management of the banks, and instead of reserving resources on a special account of the Central Bank, it is deemed more expedient that the banks maintain a certain margin on resources on corresponding accounts. If a commercial bank had an opportunity to obtain a short-term credit from the Central Bank at the expense of the reserved resources, it might also be positively perceived at the time.

In recent years, especially under conditions of global financial instability, where there are large loads of public debt in many countries and with sharp fluctuations in exchange rates. Such combinations have brought placed special importance on the operations of monetary authorities involved with securities and currency exchange in a free market system. These kinds of operations are the last facility applied in averting and economic crisis, thus heading off turmoil in the banking sector. Unfortunately, however, under conditions of rather liberalised economies, the monetary authorities are often helpless in the face of the attacks on currencies and the activities of financial profiteers. This was well-demonstrated, for example, during the financial and banking crisis faced by countries of South-East Asia in 1997-1998.

The role of the monetary and credit policy in the stock in trade of the state to regulate the economy changed depends on prevailing ideological dogmas and the actual social and economic situation.

After World War I, in the period where liberal ideology prevailed and conditions of an economic boom existed, the monetary instruments for the economy regulation prevailed over budgetary, tax and administrative mechanisms.

In addition, the crisis of the 1930s led to the re-thinking of the role of the state: monetary and credit policy lost its previous importance, and structural and institutional methods of regulation, strong budgetary policy tended to prevail.

In the late 1970s, the classical monetary school of economy revived (Fischer, Freedman and Swartz) and rates, reserve requirements, operations on the open market were offered as instruments for the economy regulation. These economists believed that the role of the state, budgetary redistribution, and taxes had to be reduced. The Ronald Reagan administration, M. Thatcher and H. Kohl governments and others added these instruments to their armoury. Consequently, monetary and credit constituents again started dominating in the economic policy framework of the majority of developed countries.

Systemic banking crises have been observed, in most developing countries and also in a number of industrial developed countries over the last two decades. They were characterised by dramatic deterioration of the assets quality and as a result – the quality of the financial performance of a large number of banks, who faced liquidity problems, loss of confidence among the population, creditors and investors towards the banking institutes of various kinds. Generally these crises were the consequence of the deterioration of the macro-economic situation, errors of the government in structural and budgetary policy, weakness of the regulatory base and supervision in the banking sector. Alongside that, the systemic banking crises had a reversal effect: frequently dramatically deteriorated the macro-economic, social and political situation.

Under such a combination of conditions as described, the goals of the monetary and credit policy are able to support the stability of the national currency, contain inflation and ensure overall economic growth. Nonetheless, under conditions of systemic banking crises, monetary and credit policy will evolve as important restructuring elements. These will in turn lead to various corrections in its objectives. Central Banks in crisis conditions often have to look for the tradeoffs in order to maintain the stability of the national currency and stabilise the banking system.

Banks essentially need additional liquid resources when faced with conditions of systemic crises, and in the majority of instances, credit institutions require short-term loans to maintain liquidity. However, there are still a significant number of banks, which have social importance, and among other characteristics, and these too could be in additional need of substantial long-term resources in order to bring about re-capitalisation and achieve financial recovery. This can be combined with the refinancing of the commercial banks on the part of the Central Bank. The purpose of such an intervention is to play a key role in overcoming the consequences of a systemic banking crisis, and it is just as important to avert it in the first place.

The modern organisation of the system of "rescuing problem banks" - and in addition to the technical subjects, a role is usually taken on by the Central Bank, in carrying out operations involving political powers of a country (the government or the legislative body). Frequently the problem is not an issue of saving a single bank but to avert the failure of the banking system as a result of multiple bankruptcies. It is clear that such operations require significant financial resources in order to have success.

The credits of the Central Bank are made available to the commercial banks on concessional conditions when pending crisis in on the horizon. For example, in Japan, the banking law (1997) allows the Central Bank to extend credits to banks that are temporarily insolvent without the requirement of providing any collateral, if they "due to accidental circumstances are unexpectedly experiencing a shortage of payment facilities" (p.33), and the Ministry of Finance may request for the Central Bank to assistance in maintaining liquidity under special conditions (in special cases if it is necessary to maintain order in the entire financial system" (p.38).

In Italy early in the 1980s, the Central Bank in compliance with a special law obtained the authorities within current monetary and credit policy to extend credits to the problem banks under subsidised interest. Such credits were particularly granted to Banco Ambrosiano and Banco di Napoli.

International practice provides many examples on how Central Banks can maintain liquidity of the credit institutions in emergency situations; however, such support does not always result in the desired result.

In Venezuela, eight banks considered solvent used special lines of liquidity of the Central Bank to cover withdrawal of deposits, but later they were unable to repay the credits provided.

In Indonesia, part of the resources of the Central Bank directed to maintain liquidity, were later converted into the public bonds among those banks receiving the assistance.

In 1991, the Bank of Finland applied a scheme when the interest rates on credits were increasing over a period of time as a mechanism to motivate the credit institutions to repay the loans as quickly as possible.

Concurrently, crediting of the commercial banks by the Central Bank under conditions of crisis an bring about an increase the rate of inflation, weaken the exchange rate of the national currency and make the crisis even harsher over the long run. It is clear, based on world practice, in order to successfully restructure the banking system, emergency credits have to be compensated by anti-inflation measures by monetary authorities.

Monetary and credit policy of the Central Bank in Malaysia provides an example of the complex approach to the restructuring of the banking system. For example, on the one hand, they restricted increase of the money supply aggregates to contain inflation, and on the other, they softened the access to credits. Credit institutions were prohibited from investing in the stocks and real estate since such investments have a tendency to quickly devaluate. The rate for refinancing was determined by the demand of the banks and real sector of the economy. At the same time, the banks (inter-bank among others) were granted credits only if they were secured loans. However, norm fluctuations for the required reserves within the day were permitted.

Central banks in other countries adjusted their monetary policy in order replenish the funds for deposit guarantees as these tended to be depleted in the presence of a systemic crisis, as demonstrated in Mexico, Venezuela, Poland and Finland.

In Sweden, to implement anti-crisis monetary and credit policy, dating back to 1993, an agency was specially set up for the sale of banks under the subordination of the Ministry of Finance aiming at providing the banks with adequate resources to replenish their capital and compensate their depositors.

Often refinancing of the problem banks on the part of the central banks was carried out not directly but via special financial institutes, as in the case of short-term crediting of the banks in Germany in order for them to maintain their liquidity, which was carried out by the resources of a special organisation "Liquidite Consortium Bank' and whose co-founder is the Bundesbank.

The law in France envisages the possibility of attracting the resources of other banks in order that Central Bank to be able to better rescue problem credit institutions.

In Russia, during 1998 banking crisis, to support current liquidity of the banking system, the Central Bank vigorously applied the policy of obligatory reserve requirements. On September 1 1998, the Bank of Russia set new levels of required reserves on deposits in Rouble and foreign currencies, and this depended on the relative share of investments of the credit institutions in the government securities (government short-term loans, federal bond loans), in functioning assets, and if the relative share was 40 percent more – 5 percent; from 20 percent to 40 percent – 7.5 percent (instead of 10 percent). For the

Savings Bank of the Russian Federation, this level was reduced to 5 percent. Along with that, due to the deposit run of the population in August-September 1998, the credit institutions had right to carry out special regulation of the obligatory reserves that allowed them to return on time the resources transferred in excess into the fund of the obligatory reserving and increase liquidity. Since 01.12.98, when the volume of obligatory reserves started to be regulated, all credit institutions had the same norm for obligatory reserves on attracted resources both in Roubles and hard currency.

The Bank of Russia also extended short term credits to the banks to maintain liquidity. Several of the large banks had been extended long-term credits for financial recovery. The collapse of the banking system was possible to avert, however, because credits were extended to the so called system creating banks, particularly to Joint-Stock Bank 'DBS-AGRO', which is later associated with various political scandals and criminal prosecutions and trials.

During the currency crisis of 1998-1999 in Georgia, the level of required reserves increased from 14 percent to 16 percent, and the National Bank of Georgia signed a special agreement (memorandum) with the leading banks of Georgia to provide financial support, if deemed necessary.

The emergency provision of credits to commercial banks under crisis conditions has been accompanied by political and economic costs in many countries.

For example, financial consequences of overcoming the crisis of Savings and Loans Associations in the US, also the discussions in regard to the efficiency and expediency of the measures to rescue problem banks led to the adoption of the Law on Improvement of the Activities of the Federal Corporation of Deposits Insurance (1991). The law determines the norms and directly prohibits the Federal Reserve System from extending emergency credit to problem banks, since it "does not encourage the stimulation of market-based self-regulation of credit institutions".

The Charter of the Central Bank of European Exchange System

also contains provisions prohibiting participation in the salvaging of problem banks.

Monetary authorities introduce changes in their policy both on the national and international levels when faced with conditions of financial globalisation and greater instability, \

<u>Under the</u> terms of General Arrangement to Borrow (GAB), some countries were able to obtain necessary resources to maintain the national liquidity (of the balance of payment) from the international organisations, particularly, from the International Monetary Fund (IMF), and under conditions of where there have been significant outflows of capital from the country. This mechanism of borrowing was not linked with common pool of fund's resources being generated as a result of membership fees, and, therefore the size of the credits was not determined by the amounts of the membership fees. Initially it was a credit union whose activities applied only to its members and the IMF could not use this mechanism to provide financial assistance to the countries experiencing hardships in terms of the balance of payments and who were not a member of the GAB. However; such automatic extension of resources was rejected and the principle of "double lock" was introduced in compliance with conditions where transaction for support required the consent of each GAB member, as well as that of the IMF. And though in 1983, the IMF obtained the right to provide credit to countries that were not members of the IMF. However, the lack of flexibility and expeditiousness in decision-making did not allow the countries, where systemic banking crisis was observed, to be able to timely obtain the necessary resources to maintain their liquidity levels.

International financial and political institutes carried out certain measures in response to the growth of financial instability, albeit the majority of experts claim that they were too late and thus ineffective. In 1995, in Halifax the leaders of "the seven" expressed concern as to the growth of instability. They proceeded to call for "initiating negotiations to double the financial resources within the GAB in order to settle emergent financial situations". It was then that New Agreement to Borrowings was signed that expanded the financial capabilities of the IMF but this did not lead to the expected qualitative improvement of the situation, neither in terms of generation of the IMF resources at the expense of obtaining loans on capital markets, or regarding the 'expeditiousness' of decision-making process.

In 1997, within the framework of the IMF, a Supplemental Reserve Facility (SRF) was established; its purpose was not to regulate the problem caused by the capital outflow, but rather to stop the outflow by bringing about a recovery of the official reserves of the country.

Inefficiency of the IMF policy observed during the crises in the countries of South-East Asia, Mexico, Argentine, and Russia. Many experts consider that this is connected with the lack of access to the resources that would be proportional to the scale of the problem; inadequacy of freedom and expeditiousness in the decision-making process, and determination in what form should the intervention actual take based concrete circumstances; lack of high quality information as a result of ineffective monitoring; and the impossibility to apply effective sanctions for the violation of established rules on the countries that borrowed the money..

The experience of the last few years demonstrates the effectiveness of the monetary and credit policy in overcoming the consequences and averting the systemic banking crises and how this depends on bringing the goals and instruments into compliance with the objectives and mechanisms of structural, institutional and tax reforms. The monetary institutes could successfully apply the instruments of monetary and credit policy in a set of measures to overcome the systemic banking crises. Concurrently, the errors in determining the strategic and tactical goals of the monetary and credit policy in the conditions of the systemic banking crises could even deteriorate the situation that is obvious on the example of Argentine and Brazil.

Taking into consideration the destructive consequences of the systemic crises, it is of utmost importance to not only fight against their consequences but to prevent them in the first place.

The following actions are assumed to increase the effectiveness of the monetary and credit policy under conditions of financial globalisation:

- to reform the system of floating exchange rates and the functions of the IMF taking into account the negative experience of the crises in South-East Asia, Turkey, Brazil, and Argentine;
- to expand the functions and responsibilities of central banks; to harmonise the monetary policy with the policy of the banking sector development;
- to study the problems of price instability, inflation, and deflation, consequences of anti-inflation policy, and price control;
- to create restriction mechanisms against the speculative movement of capital on the exchange and financial markets; and to smoothen profitability and mitigate risks in the financial and real sectors of the economy.

The adaptation of the monetary and credit policy with the realms of the financial globalisation will ensure increase in the effectiveness of not only overcoming the consequences of the systemic banking crises but to engage in preventive measure.

2.3. Institutional basis of restructuring (Taiwanese example)

A successful restructuring programme for the banking system is largely dependent on the formation of relevant institutes.

In many countries special organisations are set up for a limited period of time (4-5 years or until the end of the needed restructuring).

In a number of countries such institutes responsible for the restructuring of the banking system had been established at the Ministry of Finance.

For example, the Bank Support Authority was set up at the Ministry of Finance in Sweden. This agency had wide authorities to promote the banking system; it also had the capacity to extend credits, issue guaranties and take over banks. The government granted this agency the mandate to control the largest banks under reconstruction such as Nordbank and Gota Bank, as well as government companies who are involved in the management of the securities of Securum and Rettiva.

In Thailand, in 1977, when its systemic banking crisis was in full swing, Thailand's Financial Sector Restructuring Authority was set up in response by the Ministry of Finance. This new agency was designed and tasked with ensuring the rights of bona fide depositors and to further acts as a liquidator of insolvent banks.

Similar restructuring agencies were set up in the Czech Republic, the Russia Federation, Kazakhstan, and many other countries.

However, many other countries, especially those with a large experience of regulation of banking systems, as in the United States, have chosen a rather different approach. The entity managing the deposit insurance system in these countries became the institutional foundation for banking restructuring. This approach seems as a quite reasonable step, as the empowerment of such managing organisations, and tooled with supervisory authorities over the banks, is positioned to provide them with necessary financial support. It is also involved with selling off or merging of problem banks, their liquidation (actually a entire set of measures on restructuring) allows that not only an adequate level of firmness of the insurance systems is provided, but also significantly increases the effectiveness of the restructuring procedures. Several developing countries, particularly Taiwan, adopted lessons learned from the American practice and successfully implemented them.

The institutes for the restructuring of the banking system will be in more detail discussed on the example of Central Deposit Insurance Company (CDIC). Alongside of functioning to provide compulsory insurance of deposits, the Company carried out a number of other operations within the restructuring framework, particularly, by way of regulation of commitments of insolvent banks, as well as the provision of restricted oversight functions in the sphere of banking supervision.

CDIC was founded in 1985, and was established in compliance with the provision of the Law on Banking Activities under condition of systemic banking crises. They had become rather frequent, especially in the countries, of South -East Asia, and among others to be later described.

Take for instance, the means to restructure banks, as in the case of Taiwan, when a system of deposit insurance was introduced. The government also had the combined authority to restructure banks, and the combination of the two types of intervention has proved a successful combination, and this is also supported by international experience in other countries.

Initially, insurance in the framework of CDIC was voluntary, but at the same time the Company was liable to insure all the banks that could meet the requirements. The only incentive for the banks to become insured within CDIC system was the possibility to attract clients at the expense of an additional guarantee for the security of their deposits.

The majority of Taiwanese banks applied for and insured in CDIC. Subsequent to the amendment was introduced into the Law on the Banking Activities in 1999; all banks were required to insure their deposits in the Company. This amendment reflected world trends calling for the introduction of mandatory insurance system and assigning relevant authorities with a range of supervision, restructuring and liquidation responsibilities, among others.

Presently all banks in Taiwan must insure deposits under the CDIC framework.. This requirement is one of the many conditions along with observance of the norms for reserve limits and the provision of credits that Taiwanese banks have to carry in order to have the right to implement lawful activities within that country. If the banks fail to accomplish the above-mentioned requirements as stipulated under the agreement for insurance with CDIC, the latter has right to send a warning to a given bank with the list of measures to be applied to overcome the breach of the rules. As an extreme measure, CDIC has right to cancel the agreement and to then notify the Ministry of Finance of Taiwan. It is now possible, upon proper notification, to proceed with the option of closing the bank.

If the bank turns out to be insolvent or is on the verge of insolvency, CDIC is then appointed as an external manager of the financial institution.

The Company was founded in the format of a limited liabilities company and its authorised capital is in the ownership of the Ministry of Finance (51 percent of the share capital of CDIC) and the Central Bank of the country (approximately 49 percent). In compliance with the law, the Ministry of Finance and the Central Bank of Taiwan as founders are tasked with retaining control over CDIC.

While the Ministry of Finance of Taiwan is responsible for the regulation and supervision of the activities of the bank, bringing about their merger or affiliation, as well providing for liquidation of financial organisations within country, the Central Bank of Taiwan has the authorities to manage all-cash bid in the country, as well as to control and regulate currency.

Less than one percent of the shares of CDIC (1,000 shares out of a total of the 1 billion issued) are owned by five specially selected commercial banks. Commercial banks do not play a significant role in CDIC. They have been invited as the status of incorporators and this was only for the purpose of formally satisfying the norms of the corporate legislation of Taiwan. It is necessary for a limited liabilities company to be incorporated with not fewer than seven incorporators. The capital of the company was formed by the resources of the Ministry of Finance and the Central Bank of the country, at the same time CDIC is mandated to maintain the capital on the level of 10 billion Taiwanese dollars (approximately USD 29 million).

The Ministry of Finance and the Central Bank of Taiwan control the company's activities and appoint all members of CDIC's Board of Directors and the Ministry of Finance appoints four Board members and the Central bank a total of three.

The key function of CDIC is making sure that a deposit insurance system is implemented in the Taiwanese banks to cover possible bankruptcy of various banks. All deposits of any given bank insured upwards of 1 million Taiwanese dollars (approximately USD 29,000).

Other than providing the key function of providing deposit insurance, CDIC is also tasked with number of responsibilities in related fields: provision of banking supervision, restructuring and regulation.

The role CDIC in banking supervision is a secondary function when compared to the analogous oversight responsibilities of the Ministry of Finance and the Central Bank of Taiwan. At the same time, with the consent of the Ministry of Finance and the Central Bank of Taiwan, CDIC has the right to inspect any commercial banking instrument insured by the Company.

Upon the request of CDIC, the bank is must provide the company with all financial and commercial accounts, which includes complete information about its assets. After evaluating these documents, CDIC can send the bank a finding describing the quality of the organisation, its activities, including various recommendations on measures taken. Should the bank fails to tkae steps to follow the recommendations, CDIC proceeds to inform the Ministry of Finance and the Central Bank of the country about the identified shortcomings in the bank and may then demand relevant measures be taken to gain control over the bank.

Under conditions when the bank is experiencing financial hardships, CDIC has the right, which is based on having the permission of the Ministry of Finance to appoint its representative as a bank curator and this person will control the resolution of the deficiencies. The company can also warn the banks that are experiencing difficulties to overcome the deficiencies. However, if the bank did not fulfill this demand, CDIC can, as an extreme measure, stop the validity of the agreement on insurance and then proceed to notify the Ministry of Finance about this fact. If this is being the case, the Ministry of Finance has the right to close the bank, or to apply various restructuring schemes in bringing the bank back into normal operations.

In practice, the authorities of Taiwan usually make all attempts to avoid liquidation of the financial organisations. Preference is given to merging or affiliating the organisation experiencing financial difficulties with one or more stable financial organisations.

The amendment of the Law On the Banking Activities effective from January 1 2000, grants the Ministry of Finance of Taiwan wider authorities in regard to the assets and transactions of the financial organisations unable to carry out payments on their liabilities, also "if the depositors' interests are affected" (Law On Banking Activities, p.62).

The monetary authorities could carry out the following schemes of restructuring of a problem bank:

- discontinuation of activities or sale of the part of the bank;
- readjustment of the bank;
- suspension of the bank operations and appointment of an external administration of the bank; and
- taking other measures.

Whether the Ministry of Finance decides to restructure the bank or to appoint external administration, in both cases these duties are implemented by CDIC.

The term "restructuring" as applied in the Law of Taiwan, sounds as "reconstruction" in the translation from Chinese. The term has different from terms "liquidation" or "reorganisation" meaning. On the whole, the law of Taiwan understands restructuring as giving the bank some additional time and resources (for example, by the government) in order to bring about financial recovery. In this case, the definition of the term "restructuring" is significantly narrower than the definition usually applied in the practice of banking restructuring.

Provisions of the law on bankruptcy, reorganisation, sale on the open auctions and liquidation, as well as relevant procedures do not apply to the banks during a period of restructuring. The enforced implementation of the creditors' rights, and under conditions towards by which the obligations of the organisation subject to restructuring are secured with collateral, or whereby rights of an equitable lien as an exception to this legal requirement.

Such procedures presupposes work with assets and liabilities of the insolvent organisation and during the restructuring process, such an organisation is exempted from the repayment of liabilities and is granted protection from all requirements and outstanding claims on the part of the creditors, with the exception for the claims that were secured by the right of retention, mortgage, bond or collateral.

CDIC acquires special powers for the "clearance" of the balance sheet of the insolvent organisation as part of the process. It is vested with the specific right to review the documentation and accounts of the bank; to inventory assets, creditors, claimants and determine a list of liabilities; to hire and dismiss personnel; to purchase and sell assets; to represent the bank's interests in the court or before other organisation; to jointly manage the bank's activities.

The Ministry of Finance can apply different schemes of restructuring of the problem banks. Particularly, it can suspend the activities of the bank and appoint external administration in the face of CDIC.

In this status the Law empowers the Company to run the insolvent organisation, to withdraw stamp and accounts among others. After CDIC analyses the situation in the bank, it can state what has to be done in regard to the bank – for example, to apply merger with another more viable bank. The Company needs to get permission from the Ministry of Finance whatever decision it makes.

In case of bankruptcy of the bank, CDIC is responsible for the repayment of deposits within the norm established by the legislation in the amount of 1 million of Taiwanese dollar per one depositor. In terms of the law, the Company is liable to review the possibility of applying four possible schemes of repayment of liabilities:

- payment to the depositors;
- remittance of deposits from insolvent banks to the sound bank;
- setting control over the insolvent bank.

Before reaching a decision, CDIC is required to assess the value of each option and to choose the least costly one. If the Company decides to pay depositors, the company obtains all rights and can demand to take over the assets of the insolvent bank.

Under the banking law of Taiwan, the functions of CDIC as an agency supporting deposit insurance are combined with several auxiliary functions in the sphere of banking supervision, and the functioning of an organisation responsible for the external management and restructuring of banks. As resources in the possession of the Company are limited by the resources allocated by the Government of Taiwan through the Ministry of Finance and the countries Central, the CDIC is tasked to decide upon the least costly regulatory mechanisms in dealing with problems of insolvent banks.

As international experience demonstrates, it is expedient to set up specialised companies for the assets management. along with the institutes for restructuring. In Korea a successful restructuring of the banking system is attributed for the most part to the effective activities of Korea Asset Management Corporation (KAMCO). Comparatively, Securum and Rettiva – state companies in Sweden managing the assets effectively demonstrated, much to their advantage, successful restructuring.

Thus, the success of restructuring of the banking system not only depends on the regulated monetary and credit policy environment, and/or effective banking regulation and supervision oversight, but largely the creation of enabling institutions.

2.4. Recapitalisation of banking systems

Capital is a key indicator of the stability of any particular bank, as well as a benchmark of the entire banking system as a whole. Equity capital serves as a reserve fund for credit institution; it provides the resource for a bank's development and acts as the means of protection for its creditors and depositors from incurring losses.

In case of increased banking risks, and when faced with financial problems, it is the bank capital that suffers the most. The absolute value of the capital in problem banks, as well as being an important relative indicator – representing the adequacy of equity capital – decreases, and decapitalisation of the entire banking sector is inevitable under during banking crises, and in an environment when the number of the problem banks dramatically increases,. The capital deficit, liquidity shortage and high inherent systemic banking risks, financial stability of the banking system precariously decreases as a result.

Capital recovery is the most essential objective of the monetary authorities and those involved with debt workouts during the restructuring of any banking system. In accomplishing this objective, it is possible to apply different schemes and instruments.

Generally the state is represented in the face of the Central Bank, or under the form of a special institute that is involved in restructuring on the basis of criteria of facing the financial difficulties. Temporary administration interventions are introduced in dealing with the problem bank, much is involved here, starting out with assessing the actual financial status of the credit institution, developing a plan for its restructuring and to set up the terms to bring about the liquidation of those banks that are found impossible to restructure.

In the period from 1995 to 1997, in Mexico, National Banking and Stock Market Commission established temporary administrations to deal with medium size and small banks that held 16.5 percent of total banking assets in the country.

In Brazil in 1997, the Central Bank introduced temporary administrations in 37 commercial banks to assess their financial status and to address the possibility of their recapitalisation, which included restructuring of the problem banks, along with optimisation of their management system and practices; regulation of relations between creditors and depositors; and working with problem assets. The process also includes a set of measures for capital reconstruction. Generally speaking, it is state resources that usually serve as the main funding source for the recapitalisation of the problem banks, especially if it is temporary recapitalisation, or at least until private strategic investors become available.

For example, during the crisis in South Korea, the government took control over two large commercial banks – Korea First Bank and Seoul Bank having suffered essential losses due to the bankruptcy of the largest financial and industrial groups: Hando, Kia, Halla and Sammi. Consequently the capital of Korea First Bank comprised 2.7 percent of the total assets, of Seoul Bank – 0.97 percent, while the level defined by the law was fixed at 8 percent. The government contributed 1.5 trillion Won to each of these banks. The previous authorised capital was written off and the banks became the property of the government. The capital of other banks was increased at the expense of subscription to their subordinated capital by the government. Later, many South Korean banks were temporarily nationalised and capitalised by the government and subsequently sold off to private investors.

In Turkey, where the capital of the banking sector turned out to be significantly deteriorated, which resulted from two back-to-back systemic banking crises in a row (only about one year in between), the state programme of restructuring and recapitalisation of the banking system was adopted.

The programme was approved by the IMF and a special credit line was opened to the country in order to bring about the programme. State budgetary resources were also used in effecting the recapitalisation of Turkish banks. From 1997 to 2002, approximately USD 18 billion was spent on the recapitalisation of the Turkish banking sector. Nonetheless, as many experts considered the programme of recapitalisation in Turkey, as not having be efficient enough, the development of a new deposit insurance programme under the aegis of the IMF in 2002 was deemed necessary.

In compliance with this programme, the deposit insurance fund was granted the right to invest capital in private banks that failed to reach the capital adequacy level of 8 percent. However, recapitalisation of a private bank is permitted only if its assets comprise no less than 1 percent of the total assets of the overall Turkish banking sector..

Injection of the state resources into the capital of private Turkish banks is allowed conditional if the capital adequacy reserve levels of these banks can demonstrate positive values.

A bank with the capital adequacy ranging from 0 to 5 percent will be able to obtain state resources equally the amount of additional equity capital to by invested into the authorised capital by the main shareholder. The bank has to direct 60 percent of the invested resources into components of the real economy.

Banks with the capital adequacy from 5 to 9 percent will obtain state resources in the form of treasury securities that are convertible into stock certificates.

E. Akakoka, the head of Banking Regulation and Supervision Agency (BDDK) highlighted the importance of this programme: "The actions of the monetary authorities are aimed at observance of the standard of the capital adequacy by the banking sector in the amount of 8 percent. This programme is essential and very important for Turkey. If it is not implemented, the consequences will be outside of the framework of the responsibility of the banking sector, BDDK and the government".

During the recapitalisation of the problem banks, voluntary or enforced banking mergers are feasible. For example, in Spain, the merger during the restructuring of the problem bank may move forward if the shareholders reject the Bank's of Spain proposal to recapitalise the specific bank that incurred the losses.

Nonetheless, if the recapitalisation is not complete, the Central Bank of Spain can proceed to authorise the Deposit Insurance Fund as a source to replenish the shortfall of resources. Under such conditions such a case the Fund has the right to purchase stock of the bank in terms of the accounting value; to introduce into the bank temporary administration; in some cases to buy out sections of unprofitable loans; to decide on merging problem bank with a solvent bank that is interested in joining within the timeframe of a year.

In Mexico, Banking Commission CNBV, also is vested with the right to implement an enforced merging of problem banks as a result of restructuring. One of the following three schemes could be used:

1. Sale of the affiliated network to the commercial banks in combination with the purchase of bad assets by the Banking Fund for the Protection of Savings (FOBAPROA);
2. Partial or complete sale of all banking assets to the interested commercial banks:
3. Partial sale of the problem bank to the interested commercial banks provided that purchasers increase their share in the authorised capital in due course of time.

In compliance with the first scheme, the affiliated network of two largest banks Banca Cremi and Banca de Oriente were sold to the Spanish bank Banco Bilbao Vizcaya. The affiliations of other banks – Banco Union, Banco Interstatal and Banco del Sudeste – had been purchased by some more stable Mexican banks.

Addressing the second purchasing scheme, Banco Santander took ownership by buying 51 percent of the capital of Banco Mexicano, and the Citibank became the main shareholder of Banco Confia. Thanks to the third scheme, Canadian Bank Banco of Nova Scotia was able to purchase 10 percent of shares of Grupo Financiero Inverlat, as well as the bonds with the right to convert them into stock allowing it to increase the controlling share amount to 55 percent under the authorised capital of this Mexican bank.

Brazil found that by applying tax bonuses to encourage banking mergers some of their restructuring goals could be accomplished. Merged bank have the right to deduct the value of non-performing credits, and the merging bank obtains a credit equal to the difference between the purchase and balance sheet value of the package of stocks.

The experience of overcoming the systemic bank crises in both developed and developing countries demonstrated that effective and long-term recapitalisation of banks is feasible if the following conditions are met:

Firstly, the banks under restructuring have to immediately stop extending credits to insolvent banks

Secondly, such banks shall come up with a realistic plan of restructuring that is to be implemented under the strict control of monetary authorities.

Thirdly, the monetary authorities have to develop and strictly observe the rule of state financing of the recapitalisation programmes. Providing financial aid to the problem banks shall be strictly linked to the implementation of requirements on improving the management quality and financial status of these banks. In case the banks under restructuring violate the implementation plan and various provisions of the plan on recovery, the financial support must be reduced, and supervisory authorities have to apply punitive relevant measures to those that have violated the process.

Fourthly, responsible top management found to have been responsible for the deterioration of the stance of the bank must be immediately dismissed.

Fifthly, control over the reliability of accountability of such banks has to be tightened, as well as over the observance of established rules in regard to the capital adequacy, in particular.

2.5. Purchasing of problem assets from restructured banks by specialised institutions

The purchase of the assets from the problem banks is a widely used restructuring tool that provides for the expedient and quick resolution of the problem under conditions of liquidity shortages in the banks subject to restructuring. The most optimal way to for the government to provide the banks with adequate liquidity is to purchase the assets that have been found to not be liquid enough for that given moment. However, these must be deemed to represent real value in the future, provided that the assets are prudentially managed.

International practice clearly indicates that purchase or transfer of non-performing assets (outstanding credits, non-liquid securities and unrealisable property) which is at the disposal of specialised state organisations is not only the most widely spread practice but it also a very effective form of bank restructuring. That is the reason that special institutions had been founded in many countries, and these institutions were set up with structurally different banking systems and varying levels of economic development. Non-performing credits usually comprise the main part of the package of problem assets. Supervisory authorities consider loans that are classified by banks as being nonstandard, risky and nonperforming. The criteria for referring a loan to one or another category have are based on national peculiarities. However, in most instances, cases are defined by the conditions and circumstances of default on any loan that matured of conditions of a credit or repayment of interests, as well as the quality of the provided collateral.

The size of the non-performing credits in the banks assets is an important indicator of the banking crisis. Experts consider that if the ratio of non-performing assets to the assets exceeds 10 percent, the problems in the banking system could be classified as a full-scale crisis.

The size of this indicator during the systemic crisis largely varies by country. It equalled 50 percent in Indonesia, in the Czech Republic it was – 33 percent, USA – 28 percent, Columbia – 25 percent, Poland – 20 percent, Chile and Mexico – 19 percent, Venezuela – 15 percent, Argentine – 12 percent, Sweden and Brazil – 11 percent.

The mechanism for the purchase of the problem assets also vary, and this depends on the country; the actual practice may be either of a centralised and decentralised nature, or a combination of the two..

Decentralised method of the assets purchase is usually applied when the difficulties are experienced by relatively small number of credit institutions. Otherwise, it is common practice to set up relevant structures to manage nonperforming bank assets. Based on the experience, such a method is expedient, and especially when working with the problem credits of enterprises. It is also important to take into foremost consideration the information that the bank has about its clients. Such an approach was successfully applied at the initial stage of banking system restructuring in Sweden and later in Poland.

When the government encountered the banking crisis of 1991-1992 in Sweden, it made a plan to separate normal credits served by banks Nordbanken and Gota Bank from problem credits by founding state companies Securum and Retriva for assets management. Portfolio of problem credits of Nordbanken valued at 51 billion krona were transferred to Securum; the value of the credit portfolio of Retriva obtained as a result of transfer of problem loans of Gota Bank was estimated as high as 43 billion Krona.

Only large assets had been transferred into the state companies, and all, other problem credits below USD 1 million remained in the hands of Nordenbank and Gota Bank.

As a result, the banks under restructuring achieved an allowance of problem credits and assets, as with other Swedish banks. Later companies Securum and Retriva fell under the management of the Agency responsible for the sale of banks. The key objective of the company for managing assets was to repay the maximum possible amount of problem credits. By using either bankruptcy or other procedures envisaged by the acting legislation at the time, the companies managing the assets took over the collateral put up for the loans, including real estate objects and shares of participation in large industrial companies. Later, once the economic situation became more favourable, this property was sold by specialised companies by specialised auctions on the Stockholm stock exchange or on the open market.

Initially the government of Sweden expected that the process of assets sale would last for as long as 10 to 15 years. However, due to the general improvement in the economic situation at the national level, as well as market stabilisation, the largest portion of the assets was sold off in 1995-1996. After successful restructuring of the Swedish banking system, the companies responsible for managing the assets were liquidated in 1997.

Poland decided on a different approach, and there, companies managing the assets did so not under the status of independent legal entities were not created, but the credit institutions had to establish themselves an organisational subdivision to manage problem credits.

In terms of a centralised method of purchasing assets,, it envisages the creation of specialised corporation by the government for buying out and managing problem assets faced by the entire banking system.

In this case the assets purchased by specialised institutes from the problem banks are exchanged for debt liabilities, or traded for the stocks of the corporation that are directly managing the assets to deal with debt liabilities for the benefit of the government. The analysis of the worldwide experience demonstrates that if the hardships are experienced by a large number of banks, or when the purchased assets are somewhat homogenous, such a method of banking system restructuring is the most effective.

Moreover, as demonstrated in many countries, buying out of the problem assets in a centralised way could be implemented either by the Central Bank (Chile, Hungary, Poland), or by an Agency entrusted with restructuring (Czech Republic, USA, Mexico, and South Korea).

The choice of methods depends on the depth of the crisis and the government's financial capacity, degree of problem assets held by the banks and whether or not restructuring can be purchased either in part or completely.

The purchase of problem assets depend on the idiosyncrasies faced within a country, financial capabilities of the government, and national peculiarities of the legislation base and how this is adjusted to accommodate for specific provisions.

Take the case in 1984, the National Bank of Chile purchased risky and bad debts but did not exceed 150 percent of their capital base. At the same time, however, was that the obligatory precondition for participating in this programme was that the banks took on the obligation to service the credits and this was carried out by the National Bank during the initial stage of the crisis and in a timely fashion

During an earlier crisis in 1944 in Mexico, the Banking Fund for the Protection of Savings (FOBAPROA) would buy out problem assets only if the banks were willing to increase to their equities. The ratio between the problem assets bought out from the balance sheet of the banks and the amount paid into the authorised capital by the shareholders was 2 to 1.

In Hungary, the conditions for buying out the indebtedness were differentiated for private and government banks, and in case of the state banks, it was envisaged to purchase 100 percent of the principal and un-paid interest. Another set indicator applied for private banks: 50 percent of the assets value belonging to risky and bad liability to 1992, and 80 percent of risky and bad liability falling into this category in 1992.

During the restructuring of the credit institution, one of the problems is the assessment of the assets bought out from the problem banks. The most common method to determine current value of assets is discounting of the current value. As a rule, unsecured credits are sold at larger discounts; secured ones are assessed at higher values.

In1997, in South Korea, when faced with crisis, the Korean Asset Management Corporation (KAMCO) bought out problem credits at price comprising of 45 percent of the book value of the secured credits. A significant portion of unsecured credits were bought at significantly low prices, for 3 percent of the nominal value.

In the Czech Republic, state financial organisation Konsolidacní Banka Praha, s.p.ú. (KOB) bought out problem debts from commercial banks at fair market value (usually around 60 percent of the nominal value of the purchasing assets).

Another interesting scheme for pricing of problem assets was used in Malaysia and this applied method was referred to as adjustment of prices. And with the eventuality that the Asset Management Corporation eventually sold purchased assets at a higher price over what it paid to the bank, the banks would be refunded 80 percent of the difference.

However, in a number of countries the agencies would purchase problem credits from the banks at 100 percent of the book value.

For example, in Mexico Banking Fund for the Protection of Savings (FOBAPROA) would purchase problem assets at so called net-cost (book cost of the credit minus the cost of the set up reserve).

Assets Management Corporations could use various forms of payments while purchasing problem assets. Assets could be purchased not only by money but also paid for with bonds and bills guaranteed by the government. It is assumed that by the time of their redemption, the greatest part of the problem assets would have been already sold and the generated resources would be used to the pay the value of the redeemed securities.

The Hungarian experience demonstrated that the risky and bad debts that were purchased from the commercial bank in exchange for state bonds had a 20 year term of maturity. The yield of these instruments was linked to the yield of US treasury bills.

In providing for the exchange of 'bad' debts, Mexican commercial banks would get in exchange bills from the Banking Fund for the Protection of Savings with 10 year maturity date. The yield of these bills was set at the minimum level corresponding the rate on short-term treasury liabilities with 91-day of maturity.

Later, during the implementation process for the restructuring programme and to prevent deterioration of the financial status of the banks, it was decided that for the first three years the rate of received bills would exceed that of the treasury bills by 2 percentage points; and by 1.35 percentage points during the subsequent 7 years. All the interest accrued on the bills as the part of the restructuring programme was liable to capitalisation to economise on current budget costs and reduction of the period of the recovery of banks capital.

Along with simple purchase of problem assets, the scheme of transfer of these assets for management (trust) to the specialised companies was also applied. The Central Bank, the restructuring agency, a specialised company for purchasing assets or the bank itself could transfer the assets to the trust for management.

The advantage of such an operation is that the relations of a bank-borrower are not disrupted. Furthermore, such a decision allows the recovery of credit relations in case the debt is repaid.

A rather atypical scheme of management of problem assets was applied in Mexico, where the entire portfolio of bad debts was purchased by Banking Fund for the Protection of Savings from the commercial banks, and transferred to a trust tasked with the management of the same commercial banks. All generated funds on the part of the portfolio's management had to be applied for the repayment of the incurred liabilities to FOBAPROA.

The stimulus for these Mexican banks that were involved in vigorously selling bad and risky debts involved the introduction of financial sanctions for a delay in repayment of the bills given on exchange of problem debts. For example, if the bank is unable to repay the bill of FOBAPROA before 2005 by selling off the portfolio of bad debts, it will receive only 20-30 percent of the nominal amount of the debt as paid by the bill of exchange.

There are two key approaches to the management of problem assets base on international experience.

The first is prompt sale of the assets so not to allow further deterioration in the quality and to receive immediate financial effect in the form of additional liquid resources. Concurrently, while using this approach there is the added likelihood that the simultaneous sale of a large amount of problem assets would lead to a significant drop of their actual value. There is also a threat that problem assets would be bought at dumping price by those interested in the assets, and some actions of the people could have potentially serious political damage to the image of the company managing the assets and the institutes responsible for the restructuring.

Base upon an alternative approach, the Corporation manages the problem assets for some time, carries out presale activities, monitors the market conditions and when the assets reach the maximum price, then proceeds to gradually sell them off.

The choice of this strategy, or of the compromised one, described above, largely depends on the goals and objectives of the Corporation, the general economic situation faced in the country and severity of the banking crisis.

For example, in the US, to buy and resolve problems of doubtful debts of the credit and savings organisations Resolution Trust Corporation (RTC) was founded in 1989. The Financial Institution Reform, Recovery and Enforcement Act (FIRREA) required the Corporation to sell insolvent credit and savings organisations and their assets in such an manner that would ensure maximum amount of funds in return. A large number of insolvent organisations led to the postponement of the sale of assets and their general amount at the disposal of the Corporation continued to increase over time. In 1991, amendments were then introduced in the Act that allowed the Corporation to sell assets quicker by selling assets as portfolios in larger lots.

For the five years of existence of the Resolution Trust Corporation, the assets at the nominal value of USD 400 billion were disposed of. The amount of bad debts totally USD 8 billion was impossible to sell. The average price of sold assets was at 87 percent of their initial book value.

The experience of the Czech Republic in managing problems assets is most interesting. In the Czech Republic immediate sale of bought out assets during the banking sector restructuring was not envisaged. Part of the debt instruments and share of participation in the large Czech industrial enterprises purchased from the commercial banks by Konsolidacní Banka Praha, s.p.ú. (KOB) were transferred to the Recovery Agency founded in 1999.

The goal of the Agency was to maximise the value of the received for the management assets by conducting efficient restructuring and revival of industrial enterprises for their further sale to the strategic investors. Due to the complexity of the targeted tasks, the Agency had attracted the private structures (consortium in the composition of Lazard and Latona) to be responsible for managing its current activities and developing plans for the companies being restructured. However, the law did not grant the Agency broad authorities in managing the problem assets.

For example, The Agency did not have special authorities (except for the general rules set by the Civil Code of the Czech Republic) to investigate and recognise as void suspicious transactions on withdrawal of assets. On the whole, the recovery and further privatisation of the banking sector in the Czech Republic were considered successful. However, the revival of the largest industrial enterprises did not achieve anticipated results. Therefore, in 2001 the government of the Czech Republic decided to liquidate the Recovery Agency.

As the analysis of the international experience demonstrates, the corporations for assets management used diverse procedures for collection of problems debts. The following was most widely applied:

- open auctions for sale of the problem assets;
- bankruptcy of debtors;
- debts restructuring;
- attracting the private specialised organisations to manage and sell assets.

In the countries, where the law allowed the corporations to exercise wider authorities in choosing the means for assets sale, many different mechanisms were used.

For example, Regulating Trust Corporation in the US permitted the buyers to return the purchased assets for the purpose of refinancing (usually completed) during a preliminary pre-defined period of time. Such a method of assets purchase was conditional by the fact that perspective buyers spent a considerable amount of time assessing the quality of the large packets of assets and aspects for the complex structure being offered for sale.

While using the above-mentioned technology in purchasing assets, the conditions varied, and the degree depended on the type of assets offered for sale. However, on average the legitimate return of the purchase assets within a year was possible. In actual practice, only one-third of sold off assets under the described scheme was returned by the buyers.

Based upon another category of scheme, the Resolution Trust Corporation extended a loan for buying problem assets.

The Resolution Trust Corporation vigorously applied securitization of unorthodox types of assets in the final stage of its activities, as was the example of mortgage credits. A pool of homogenous credits would be formed that would afterwards was transferred to the trust fund to support the issuance of secured certificates supported by this pool. Overall, the total of mortgage credits valued at USD 42.2 billion was securitised.

Experts describe the mechanism of securitization as a mechanism that allowed the companies involved in the trust to work in limited time restraints and how they were able to sell a significant amount of mortgage credits at an otherwise higher price than if the credit had been sold on an individual basis.

Another example of where securitization of assets was successfully applied was in Korea during a period of banking restructuring. The attributed success under restructuring and securitization was promoted by the creation of a system of institutes that worked with purchasing of assets, management of assets, and insurance of risk and the subsequent issuance of securities.

Assets management corporations were, as a rule at the international level, set up for the period of restructuring of the banking system; the terms of their activities significantly varies in different countries. In the Czech Republic the Recovery Agency functioned for three years, Swedish Agency of Support to Banks – for 5 years, Resolution Trust Company in the US – less than 6 years. However, this was not always true. In a number of countries the above-mentioned structures had been retained.

For example, in South Korea and Thailand Assets Management Agency acquired new authorities and continues to function.

Purchase of problem assets along with recapitalisation of credit institutions is considered as the least painful form of restructuring. However, such restructuring form cannot always be applicable for problem banks. There are two main reasons: firstly, it requires a significant financial investment which is not always available. Secondly, financial status of a problem bank are often so depressing that are no other ways to restructured than in 'hard form'.

Moreover, under conditions when recapitalisation or financial aid to a problem credit institution or insolvent bank by the purchasing of problem assets is not acceptable, and because of various considerations other forms of restructuring are applied, such as amicable settlement or liquidation of the insolvent institution.

2.6. Amicable settlement with creditors as alternative to liquidation and a mechanism of problem bank restructuring

Such a type of restructuring implies the presence of effective liquidation procedures for insolvent banks and the real possibility to revive a bank by making an amicable settlement with its creditors, and this is in spite of the fact that mechanisms used in the regulation of insolvent banks vary from country-to-country, it is still one of the effective measures to bring about debtor's restructuring, and foresee a procedure to reach an amicable settlement.

National legislations should be taken into consideration, especially in terms of the peculiarities that the banking sector and how this impacts the effectiveness of different approaches towards the amicable settlements and bankruptcies.

Bankruptcy and Insolvency Act in Canada does not apply to banks. Instead, Winding-Up and Restructuring Act is the document that controls credit institutions and regulates amicable settlement procedures as applied to banks.

Law on Banks and Savings Banks (Loi fédéral sur les banques at les caisses d'épargne) sets a number of special norms applied towards insolvent banks and in some cases compounds the norm of general act on bankruptcy.

Amicable settlement for companies and commercial banks is regulated by the same category of legislation in Belgium, Spain and Singapore. In Belgium – the Law on Judicial Settlement (Loi relative au concordat judiciaire) and Law on Bankruptcy (Loi sur les faillites), in Spain – Commercial Code and Law on Payment Suspension, in Singapore – Law on Companies.

In a number of countries (Argentine, Italy and Belgium) amicable settlements could be concluded only if a legal entity has not yet been recognised as being bankrupt.

In Belgium conciliation procedure (analogy of the amicable settlement) is an alternative to bankruptcy. This restructuring form could be initiated towards a bank provided that it is temporarily unable to accomplish its obligations or if the financial status will prevent it from from doing so anytime in the nearest future, and thus it is expected could lead to non-fulfilment of one's obligations. Specifically, this is the case when there is a decrease in the value of net assets below the predetermined level based on the law, and the threshold criterion to be deemed as being an unsatisfactory financial status. Conciliation procedure applies if the court assumes the possibility of financial supporter of the debtor.

The situation differs in Canada and the Netherlands, where the amicable settlement between a bank and its creditors can be only be reached under bankruptcy proceedings and in such an instance concluding an amicable settlement shall only be reviewed before the court under the same process as when the decision to liquidate the insolvent bank was first reached When this is the case, and as a result of achieving an amicable settlement, the bankruptcy procedure is most often discontinued.

In spite of the legislation of various countries, their differences, the actual procedure for amicable settlement are very much alike. A bank or a supervisory body submits an application to the court requesting for a friendly and mutually agreed settlement. The application has to contain the motive for the debtor's action, brief analysis of its financial status and listed advantages for the creditors and the bank itself. A financial statement and a copy of the creditors' register are attached to the pending application.

The court then assesses the prospects in terms of the recovery of debtor's financial standing and ways to achieve solvency and what would then be necessary to settle. However, if there a lack of justification exists for the purposed amicable settlement, the court will proceed to satisfy the bank's request or that of the supervisory body, and in follow up, will authorise a special attorney to be appointed in order to supervise the implement its decision. Such an attorney, even with legal standing is not in the position to remove the bank's management body and assume control over banking activities. This person does have the legal right to take all the necessary measures in bringing about the execution of a deal or effecting other actions that would otherwise inflict damage the on the lender.

In the majority of the countries a moratorium to satisfy the requirements of creditors could be introduced under the terms of conditions of concluding and executing an amicable settlement.

In practice the settlement's conditions could envisage a debt relief, deferment of payment or both options simultaneously. In a number of countries the law allows transfer of a part of the debtor's property or his stocks or debt liability as a smart-money to the creditors.

The settlement decision is made at the creditors' meeting by the casting of votes. Then the amicable settlement reached by creditors must be further approved by the court. The court must be satisfied that all legal norms have been followed to as part of the decision-making process.

In a number of countries, for example, in Australia and Switzerland, the court has the right to introduce some amendments and possible innovations that the court may deem as necessary into the terms of the settlement that has already been approved by the creditors'.

Also, the right to reject the amicable settlement can be based on the following:
- the payment to the creditors envisaged by the settlement does not comply with the debtor's financial capabilities;
- the provisions of the settlement infringe upon the rights of at least some part of the creditors;
- the creditors' decision on the approval of the amicable settlement was influenced by fraudulent practice.

The amicable settlement approved by the court is mandatory for all of the creditors.

Many problems arise during the approval of the amicable settlement. Firstly, it refers to the determination of the groups (category) of creditors. Such categorisation into groups is acceptable in as standard international practice, and if the creditors have various legal interests calling for principally different approaches, there is the possibility of dividing creditors into different groups as envisaged under the legislation of Argentine, Belgium, Great Britain, Germany, Spain and many other countries.

And yet, in Australia, for example, the amicable settlement is reached without dividing the creditors into groups.

In Germany, the creditors with the largest volume of claims and bank employees are identified as separate categories.

In Spain, the creditors during the amicable settlement in compliance with the local legislation are divided into three groups:

1 group – employees of the company-debtor, tax and social payment creditors;

2 group – creditors whose claims are secured by collateral;

3 group – the rest of the creditors.

A separate group affords creditors certain privileges in satisfying their claims. Generally the claims of such category of creditors are satisfied at full determined amount. There also might be such an instance when the provisions of the amicable agreement do not apply to such a category of creditors.

In the Netherlands, the creditors of secured debts and tax or other compulsory payment creditors are not covered by terms of the amicable settlement.

In Denmark, the provisions of the settlement may not apply to the creditors' claims not exceeding the identified minimum level. Normally, these claims are fully satisfied before the settlement is actually concluded.

Concurrently, according to the Swiss legislation, for example, creditors-physical persons do not form a separate group during the process of an amicable settlement and legal norms applicable to the legal entities are also contingent upon them.

Payment amounts to creditors are based on the terms of the amicable settlement, which in turn depends on the financial status of the debtor. However, the following principle always holds true: payments made under the settlement shall not be less than what envisaged by the provision of the liquidation..

In some countries acting legislation determines the minimum payment. In Denmark, for instance, the amicable settlement has to satisfy at least 25 percent of the creditors' claims. Debt relief of more than 75 percent is permissible only in extreme situations and only with the court's permission. In Italy and Argentine, the creditors' claims during the amicable settlement must be satisfied at a level of at least 40 percent of those involved.

Furthermore, courts in all countries could repudiate the approval of the amicable settlement if the court would conclude that the debtor's property significantly exceeds the claims in compliance with terms of the amicable settlement, and the case shows an unjustified writing-off of greatest part of the debt.

Any such settlement shall be considered as approved, when the majority of the creditors voted in agreement. In some countries simple majority suffice, in others – a qualified majority. In countries, as in Spain, for example, where the creditors are classified into groups, the voting takes place on a group-by-group basis. When this is the case, approval is required, and this is to be obtained separately for each individual creditor group.

In Argentine, the amicable settlement is considered as approved when the absolute majority of creditors of both the total overall number and allocated within the majority of each of the voting group voted for its favour.

In Canada, the amicable settlement is reached only when all the bank's creditors and among particular groups have agreed. At the same time, the settlement is concluded when 75 percent of the creditors attending the meeting voted for it.

The number of votes is determined as proportional to the size of the claims towards the bank, as most often practice is in the international experience. Other countries have a combined system is applied, and when the votes are counted to see whether the amicable settlement is approved or not, the majority of votes defined by the number of creditors and the majority of votes calculated by the volume of claims are both determined in the final counting. Such a system is used in Germany, Belgium, Italy and the Netherlands.

In the vast majority of countries, the amicable settlement must be approved at least by 60 percent of the creditors who take part in the voting. If in this case, the debt relief comprises more than 60 percent, to approve the amicable settlement to be reached, the number of votes can be no less than the amount required for approval.

In Germany, those creditors voting settlement do so by different categories. Like with most countries, decision are considered as agreed if majority of the creditors, both by the actual number and the volume of claims for each group votes in favour. However, still court maintains the right to approve the amicable settlement, and even under conditions that not the majority of creditors of the group voted in favour, and this is possible when it is assumed that the creditors' condition of this group would be such that the satisfaction of their claims would not deteriorate in case of the liquidation of the bank, and considering the prospect that the majority of the voting groups supported the amicable settlement.

In Switzerland, the peculiarity of the amicable settlement lies in the following: only those creditors taking part in the voting, who are not in favour and this is determined at the creditors' meeting, if less than the required number is available to approve the amicable, then a settlement is not concluded. The creditors are under the terms to become familiar with the draft settlement at all bank branches, and their addresses are published in official publications.

To show disagreement with the draft amicable settlement, the creditor could go to any published addresses or directly to the special attorney and put one's signature in a special list to showing the special exceptions made. All such objections posed by the creditors are evaluated by a special attorney. The settlement's terms are considered as disapproved by the creditors, if more than one third of the total number as listed in the register objected. Certainly, this group of creditors has to own more than the third of the total claims towards the bank-debtor. Otherwise it is assumed that the creditors have given their approval to the amicable settlement.

Meanwhile, in light voting procedure, in all countries, any amicable settlement approved at the creditors' meeting and endorsed by the court, which is a mandatory requirement for the creditors and without there being any exception. It is also important to note that if the concluded settlement is not approved, that the next stage is for the initiation of the liquidation process.

The institute for concluding amicable settlement under certain conditions could be an effective instrument applied to problem bank restructuring. However, it calls for special caution, as despite a number of economic advantages (recovery of the bank's functioning, time to work on problem assets), there are some moral problems – at least parts of the creditors capitulate to the will of the majority creditors.

2.7. Liquidation as a form of restructuring of problem banks

The form of restructuring that gets applied to a credit institution depends on a number of circumstances. Firstly, it is determined by the availability of financial resources to the stakeholders involved in the restructuring process. A key participant of the banking sector restructuring, as a rule, is the government, and this especially the case at the operational stage of overcoming the banking crisis. However, the financial capabilities of the state are determined by the budgetary condition, macroeconomic situation and political factors of the country. It is not always possible for the government to have access to sufficient resources for the restructuring - this is especially true in the case of developing countries and those in transition.

Many gradual forms of restructuring (recapitalisation and problem assets management) along with injecting essential financial resources into the insolvent banks calls for a relatively long period of time. There are, however, various political and social conditions (for example, concentrated pressure from the creditors or criticism of the restructuring programme from the opposition), or limitations as monetary authorities may not have even have resources available in the short-term.

Furthermore, delays are often related to problems in the banks, and these have been neglected (for example, if the interfering of the supervisory authorities has been rather drawn-out), and gradual forms of restructuring fall short in bring about rehabilitation and thus bankruptcy is inevitable.

In all of the abovementioned cases (or in a combination thereof), the only feasible way to restructure is liquidation. Often, the monetary authorities start out by using gradual forms of restructuring but are not confident in whether they will be efficient or not , and the alternative to proceed to the liquidation of the banks and bankruptcy proceedings.

The international experience under such circumstances offers a wide range of instruments to bring about bank liquidation and starting out with common procedures of bankruptcy under a single law that cover all types of enterprises, and starting with banks and concluding with "administrative" system that envisage alternatives to the use court based bankruptcy operations.

Below, one can find the review of a number of liquidations systems of credit institutions having both advantages and disadvantages.

2.7.1. Argentine

Under conditions when the financial recovery of a problem credit institution (including the cases when the credit institution had not submitted a plan for the financial recovery, or if that plan is not implemented) and it is impossible, the Central Bank of Argentine will move to revoke the licence that had been provided that credit institution.

In general, prior to revocation, the decision is reached by the regulatory organisation for the structural reorganisation of the credit institution and this decision envisages recapitalisation of the credit institution or the application of a mechanism involving the transfer of assets and liabilities to institutions.

Those credit institutions receive those assets and liabilities are decided by the Central Bank, and upon receiving the assets and liabilities, the organisation establishes a Trust Fund in order to manage the assets. The specially established trust fund issues two types of bonds so to partially cover the risks of the recipient credit institution,. The first type bonds are transferred to the bank-recipient, and other types of bonds are bought out by the Deposit Guarantee Fund (SEDESA). The ratio of issuing bonds of types 1 and 2 are calculated in a manner that the expenses of SEDESA are less than if a credit institution had been liquidated. The size of the deposits subject to insurance is also taken into consideration. Those deposits not exceeding 30 thousand pesos are secured in Argentine.

The credit institution whose assets and liabilities have been transferred and afterwards liquidated, is done by a liquidator who, as a rule, appoint to oversee the transfer of the assets and liabilities to other credit institution, and this agent virtually always initiates the bankruptcy procedure. The actual application calling for the recognition of the credit institution as bankrupt is either submitted by the Central Bank or the creditors.

Supervision over such bankruptcy procedure is in compliance with the general Law On Bankruptcy and oversee by a bankruptcy court for the credit institutions. The Central Bank lacks authority in terms of supervision over this process and does not interfere.

2.7.2. Spain

The Bank of Spain has the authorisation to send its employees as inspectors of crisis banks with the right to "veto" any management decisions, control the activities of temporary managers, and replace them, if deemed necessary.

The decision on liquidation becomes valid after the approval of the agreement on the liquidation of the credit institution. Such a decision is concluded by ¾ of the total number of creditors present at the creditors' meeting (or by absentee voting), in case the so called procedure of the payment suspension determines that such a recovery is not feasible.

An agreement for liquidation is the basis to revoke a banking licence belonging to the credit institution. Generally the liquidation results from concluding an agreement with the creditors during the period when payments are suspended. The liquidation under such terms is favourable for the bank and creditors alike. The advantage of the payment suspension to the usual bankruptcy procedure is that it is fast and more completely satisfies the creditors' needs.

The liquidation commission formed by creditors is responsible for the liquidation process, and this is effective by making settlement with the creditors and in the following priority order: covering of payment for salaries and wages and other employee allowances, social payments; tax payments; payments to creditors with collateral (payments are to made against collateral); to those the creditors that submit official documents – court decision, legal decision, etc; payments to the promises; payments to remaining creditors.

The legislation envisages protection of creditors' interests from fraudulent actions of the administration of the credit institution during the liquidation process. All the property transactions carried out in 15 days prior to the liquidation are automatically cancelled. Mortgage transactions and transactions with collateral are closely examined. When liquidation decision on for the credit institution is concluded, the court still has the option to annul long-term property transactions.

A credit institution is also subject to liquidation if it is recognised as being bankrupt.

The decision on bankruptcy is made by the court upon the creditors or the credit institution's statement to that effect. Any such statement could be submitted to the court any time, and this is whether or not the liquidation procedure (procedure of payment suspension) has been instituted against the credit institution. At the time that a court opens a bankruptcy suit, other proceedings related to the credit institution are stopped. And if the court recognises the credit institution as being bankrupt, bankruptcy proceedings are then initiated in follow-up.

According to Spanish experts, liquidation under conditions of bankruptcy is the less desirable method. It is a long and drawn out process and costly for all parties involved. Much money must be spent on legal proceedings and other payments for the services of intermediary companies' services. As a result there are less resources available in the final stage to satisfy various outstanding claims.

2.7.3. Poland

The Commission for Banking Supervision as established in Poland has the right to go to court with the request to instigate the bankruptcy procedures. There isn't any other body or legal entity has the right to apply to the court with for this purpose.

The executive body of the Commission for Banking Supervision is the General Inspectorate of Banking Supervision, and upon application to the court by this body, the bank's activities are suspended other than for passive transactions. However, the banking licence is not revoked until the court recognises the bank as being bankrupt.

The legal entity, including the bank, is considered bankrupt, if it fails to meet the creditors' claims but prior to the court deciding on the recognition of the bank as being bankrupt, it requires pertinent conclusion of specialists. The property is assessed by independent experts who are on the register in the Ministry of Justice.

On the day when the bank is declared bankrupt, the employees of the General Inspectorate of Banking Supervision, together with the employees of the bank carry out an inventory of the bank's property, and the managers are responsible for the preparation of the balance sheet of the bank within a two-week term, that period starts on the date the bank's activities were suspended.

As soon as the decision about the bankruptcy is made, the Board of Directors of the bank is being liquidated; all its members are discharged from their activities. The court assigns the authorised person to carry out the bankruptcy procedures and either a legal entity or a physical person can be assigned to be an authorised person for such an action..

There are certain restrictions as the kind of persons who could be assigned as an authorised person. For example, a specialist of the National Bank of Poland could not be an authorised person. The activities of the authorised person are under the control of a court that can replace this individual at any time. Furthermore, the authorised person is accountable to the Commission for Banking Supervision.

In a month's time the authorised person has to draw up a list of creditors, which is then transferred to the Bank Guarantee Fund

The fundamental goal of the authorised person is to sell the bank as a whole. The person prepares a conclusion and submits it to the Commission for Banking Supervision.

If there are several candidates willing to purchase the bank as a whole, it is left to the court to select the buyer. Only a bank can be buyer of the institution to be sold, and if there isn't any buyer who would be willing or able to purchase the bank as a whole, the property of the bank is sold off, part-by-part, i.e. as stipulated under bankruptcy procedures.

Unlike bankruptcy, the liquidation of the bank is initiated when the losses exceed 50 percent of the total value of the equity capital.

Any decision on liquidation is concluded by the Commission for Banking Supervision that determines all the details involved under liquidation procedures and this is realised either by selling the bank as a whole or part-by-part.

The Commission assigns a liquidator, defining the assigned rights and duties and controls the individual's actions. Under conditions that the liquidator has violated some aspects of the assigned duties, as stipulated under the rights of the Commission, a replacement can be found. The activities of the liquidator are under the control of the court, and yet the court controls the initial appointment.

The liquidator proceeds to submit a balance sheet to the Commission as of the date when the bank's bankruptcy was declared and when confirmed by the auditor.

The liquidator assesses the value of the bank, which is calculated on the basis of the value of each stock. The bank value is discussed by the liquidator and the buyer, and if the worth of the stock is a negative figure, the costs for the liquidation procedure should also be determined, and provided that the price of the stock comprises a positive value, the price is stated, beginning with shareholders' interests and subjected to liquidation costs. Usually two expert-evaluators are invited to take part in such a procedure.

In addition, even before the Commission for Banking Supervision fixes a date for instituting the liquidation process,] information is kept in secret or the sake of confidentiality. Subsequently the Commission reviews the candidate banks that are under consideration as potential buyers for purchase the credit institution being liquidated.

If the Board of Directors disagrees with the Commission's resolution it has the option of taking them matter to court and until at such time as the court is able to decide the matter, the bank's pending sale is held in abeyance and the sale cannot proceed. Upon a legal decision, any appeal must be submitted within a period of 7 days.

Until at such time that the liquidation decision is confirmed the bank continues to carry out transactions, and upon a decision, the Commission for Banking Supervision proceeds to make a public announcement about the liquidation of the bank using the media. This is the time when most clients will discontinue making deposit in the banks being liquidated. The information is to be printed in the main newspaper two times within a period of one month. A list of all the liabilities of the bank is attached to purchase contract, and money payable on call deposits can be paid to the clients any time. As for other deposits, 50 percent of the principal is paid, and it is to be noted the interest is still being accrued but not credited for payment.

The resources designated for the repayment of the creditors are kept in a special deposit account for 5 years, and only then can be transferred into the reserve fund of the Banking Guarantee Fund.

2.7.4. Belarus

According to the law of Belarus "On the National Bank of the Republic of Belarus", the right to decide an enforced liquidation of banks, branches under the status of a legal entity, including representative branches of foreign banks is granted to the National Bank of Belarus.

A decision to liquidate is possible under the following conditions: if the bank delays the beginning of its planned activities for a period lasting longer than six months from the moment of it legal registration, violates the law of the Republic of Belarus, its charter, and instructions of the National Bank. In addition, if it is revealed that the insurance of the licence was based on incorrect information, and if the bank submitted for a second time an incorrect report, which concealed the bank's actual financial situation.

The decision on the enforced liquidation of the bank is concluded the Management of the National Bank, and as soon as such decision is reached, the National Bank enters into the Single State Register of Legal Entities information that confirms that the bank is under liquidation procedures.

To bring about the liquidation, the Chairperson of the Management of the National Bank assigns a special liquidation commission, and those that are assigned to this body, shall not be less than 5 in number. National Bank employees and other banking representatives, tax authorities, state bodies, such as social security, employment committees under the Ministry of Labour, local administration, creditors, various founders, labour organisations, law enforcement bodies, and other responsible control agencies must agree with these agencies as to implementing the decision to close a bank under conditions as described.

Upon the appointment of a commission, authority is given for to take over the responsibility for running the bank. The commission is accountable to, and under control of the National Bank, until such time as the actual liquidation of the bank has been realised.

In organising the work required to complete the bank's liquidation, the plan must be approved by
National Bank and its approval must be secured with the accompanying actual timeline that will be applied use in achieving the final result.

The liquidation commission is vested with the responsibility for analysing the financial standing of the bank, and if the bank does not have sufficient resources and property, as necessary to fully satisfy the creditors' claims, the liquidation commission is obliged to apply to the economic claims court pursuant the bank's bankruptcy, and the time allowed for this application to be made is within a month from the moment the decision for the forced liquidation was first concluded.

Provided that the economic court declares the bank bankrupt, those authorities for the bank's liquidation are assigned from the special commission and by the National Bank, shall appear before the liquidation commission as was established by the court. The composition of the liquidation commission is essentially the same and is made up of employees of the National Bank.

A proxy (an administrative receiver) in the proceedings on economic insolvency and bankruptcy could be either in the form of a physical person or a legal entity. The proxy (receiver) is the head of the liquidation commission. The receiver is obliged to have an obtained a licence issued by the Committee on Reorganisation and Bankruptcy at the Ministry of State Property Management and Privatisation. The control over the bankruptcy procedure is conducted by the judge of the economic court who regularly hears liquidation commission findings and (without convening the session), and adopts concrete decision on various issues connected with force liquidation, as may be necessary.

2.7.5. United States

The initial stages related to liquidation of problem banks is maintained under the control of the Exchange Control Agency, particularly, of the special supervision branch which is responsible for monitoring the banks based on set standards and are expected to proceed to bankrupt within a year or two.

Once a bank is designated as a problem bank, a special group will be assigned the task of supervision, consisting of a group of experts. They will be provided with information collected by banking regulators and this may be those working for regional subdivisions of the Exchange Control Agency that are responsible for carrying out technical inspection of problem bank, as well as those who are directly under the bank's management. Meanwhile, the information is disseminated weekly, and in certain cases even on a daily basis.

At the initial stage, the problem bank receives supervisory directions in terms of the things that the bank is required to do in order to attract new capital, adjust its credit policy, and form additional reserve funds as necessary to for losses on loans, and to replace management staff. In practice, however, such measures often bring no results and the problem bank proceeds to bankruptcy.

In such instances, the Exchange Control Agency has the authority to assign a liquidator in the bank under the auspices of the Federal Deposit Insurance Corporation.

An early warning system that provides for early intervention in the affairs of credit institutions is in place and has been functioning for many years in the United States. Early intervention implies development of an adjustment programme which is aimed at reducing the probability of bankruptcy of credit institutions. In the eventuality, however, and despite these measures, failure would then occur, the liquidation process for the now insolvent credit institution is then executed.

The liquidation of the insolvent credit institutions is carried out by the Division of Resolution and Receiverships that has was set up by the Federal Deposit Insurance Corporation back in 1991.

In legal terms, 90 days is allocated to bring about a bank's liquidation. However, in practice it lasts on average for 110 days, and to extend the term of the process, official permission must be requested.

Upon the receipt of official notice from the agency having issued the banking licence, or from the Supervisory Division as to the pending liquidation of a credit institution, the planning group discusses with the bank management organisational issues, the structure and integrity of the assets and liabilities, among others. A group of specialists (from 5 to 25 people depending on the composition of the assets portfolio and urgency of the liquidation process) is sent to the bank after having reviewed banking asset information as well as other accounts. The group then proceeds to draw up a report describing the valuation of the assets that are of a descriptive nature. However, this is an internal document and is not shared with potential buyers.

The concept of liquidation is developed on the basis of the above-mentioned documents, and the following factors are taken into consideration:

- type and quality of assets;
- importance of the deposit base for the potential buyers;
- interest of the potential buyers.

The decision largely depends on the current demand and competition on the market, and takes into consideration the restructuring of a credit portfolio,

There are a number of ways for the liquidation of a bank:

- purchasing of assets and assuming the liabilities (sale of the bank as a whole);
- purchasing of assets and assuming the liabilities and allocating the losses;
- purchasing of assets and assuming the liabilities (separate groups of assets);
- transferring of insured deposits.

When the bank is sold as a complete package, its' gross assets and liabilities are transferred to the buyer. An exception could be applied in the event that the assets are connected with illegal activities; and when there has been a conflict of interest between some parties and even in instances when the liquidator is somehow an interested stakeholder. Other examples may be when there are outstanding loans to directors and the bank's management; and, various assets affected by environmental problems.

The sale of particular groups of assets allows flexibility by selling assets to a number of buyers. Package of assets is offered at set price; and the buyers could receive them along with the packages of deposits or separately. The possibility of splitting up the assets allows for the separation of subsidiaries, and to obtain competing purchase proposals from consortiums of buyers.

The division of losses has been historically applied during the liquidation of large credit institutions. Those unrecoverable credits are divided between Federal Deposit Insurance Corporation and the buyer at the ratio of 80 to 20 percent.

Allocation of losses allow for a reduction in costs by the insurance fund as the largest part of the assets still remain in the private sector. In addition, negative consequences for the regional economy are also reduced.

The preparation to the closure of the bank starts along with the actions for the bankruptcy resolution. Necessary information is being collected, the status of the assets and deposits of the bank is being assessed and organisational measures are being prepared.

The closure involves:

- ensuring security of the organisation, its assets and documentation;
- preparing notices to the stakeholders;
- taking an inventory of the assets and liabilities of the credit institution;
- preparing the balance sheet that reflects all assets and liabilities;
- preparing to repay depositors;
- identifying potential claims;
- developing an action plan to the employees' rights and privileges.

To ensure the integrity of banks, security companies are called in to make sure that locks are replaced, modes of communication are protected from the possibility of any unsanctioned access, and transactions via cash machines dispensers are ceased. These expenses are incurred by the liquidator (i.e. Federal Deposit Insurance Corporation).

Insight into the international liquidation experience gained with the experience of credit institutions further demonstrates that any effective system for the sell-off of financial institutions involve the following components:

- A legislative system that establishes relevant parameters controlling the activities of the credit institutions;
- Effective supervisory system allowing for the state to track financial status and stability of the credit institutions;
- System ensuring execution of set norms that avert risky, illegal and other forms of malpractice that increase bankruptcy threats;
- Clear legal norms and procedures that set forth the conditions and mechanisms for the liquidation of failed banks.

Considering that direct liquidation is not always the most effective preference, it is important to be in the position to weight the relative advantages and disadvantages of the different options (recapitalisations, mergers and takeovers, and the purchase of problem assets).

This raises issues as to how the direct and indirect costs on liquidation of the bank will be distributed among the state, guarantee fund, creditors of insolvent bank and other legal entities, which are also important factors to take into consideration. Obviously the more complete the set of alternatives for the disposal by relevant government authorities, the higher the likelihood that the most optimum restructuring plan that addresses the moral and financial costs for all stakeholders to the will be applied.

2.8. Creating an effective risk management system in commercial banks as a basis for averting systemic banking crises

World experience effectively demonstrates that effective bank restructuring involves the establishment of stable mechanisms to deal with the adverse external effects, and in the absence, it is impossible to subject the banking system and its management to qualitative changes. It is not by happenstance that the recent initiatives of the Basel Committee and the introduction of a number of innovations into the banking regulation by various developed countries, particularly in the US, are designed to intentionally extend additional rights to the banks, thus enabling them to exercise more responsibility over the quality of their management and control over banking risks.

Any risk management system that is relevant to the threats of global financial instability must be formed in the banks of developed and transitional countries, and that includes Georgia among others.

Complex risk management and internal control of commercial banks, provided that they are adequately organised and efficient, will allow them to compare risks as part of the decision making process and to implement banking activities, thus successfully overcoming systemic crises and minimising related losses. Any complex management system over banking risks is characterised by establishing and improving the system of norms, and that includes the tracking and supervisory system.

For Georgia, commercial banks have access to a tracking system that fulfils the demands of the National Bank of Georgia (NBG), as well provides a system of internal control in providing for an operative response to emerging problems. The efficiency of the risk management system is demonstrated by quantitative indicators and the fulfilment of established norms, as well as the degree of effectiveness demonstrated with immediate responses when faced infringements by commercial banks. The existing risks and norms are in place and have been designed to circumvent a systemic banking crisis.

Many problems emerge in the process of establishment such a complex risk management system as a hedge in averting possible banking crises. For example, how best to select the sources for financial resources, to manage bank operatively, its corresponding accounts, assets and resources, and the management of bank specific risks a banking undergoing restructuring – tax risks, guarantee risks, etc.

It is important to divide the analysis in two directions, as in the case of commercial banks, and among those normally functioning banks that are not a subject of restructuring, and, for those banks being prepared for restructuring or those in the process of restructuring.

Meanwhile, the general problem is making the transition to advanced automated informational-analytical systems and complexes, thus allowing for more comprehensive and in-depth analysis. It is necessary to know what kind of problems may arise during the complex formation process of risk management.

Take for instance, in the absence of a number of necessary normative documents in being able to determine how to calculate and identify the extent of the risk; what is necessary in creating reserves for active transactions of the bank – transactions on receivables, factoring and leasing, while they do exist in accounting. In other words, in terms of a number of issues, there is a total lack of normative documents or event currently existing normative acts that call for improvement to be implemented.

Now to look at the problems involved in the functioning of commercial banks.

It is because of the absence of a clear methodological basis, that internal control services for the proper functioning are uncommon for this service as in the case of providing written methods for the range of other services in the bank. Internal control must be under the control of defined written auditing methods, i.e. definition of means, types of audits, delineation the list of documents that is to be applied during the audit. However, the service of internal control shall not have to implement other banking services.

The next barrier hindering formation of a banking risk management system is ambiguity of both current and strategic objectives for development of the bank.

Furthermore, the problem also lies in the level of quality of the risk evaluation and control, and unclear functions often leading to inadequate coordination of work between various subdivisions.

To insure the success of the process for creating the banking risk management system, it is important that the bank employees consciously apply standards, well-developed methods and procedures for internal control and internal audit and that these applied to all banking subdivisions.

Often the banks do not allocate functions and duties between the services of the internal control and audit. It is important to remember that internal control is placed on the formation of audit system, regulation and evaluation of banking risks in order to minimise losses emerging from banking activities and making effective managerial decisions. Internal audits are, in the first instance, periodical and provide for an independent evaluation of the controlling system.

In a number of cases, introduction of double-checks (simultaneous and follow-up control) in the commercial banks is necessary. It is also important to establish an interconnection between them, as well as between the subdivisions carrying out controlling operations. However, this does not happen when there is a shortage of risk management specialists and the absence of services controlling risks in the various bank branches.

Furthermore, by not having special indicators to measure the effectiveness of the internal control mechanisms for particular checking and this is made the all more difficult because of undeveloped criteria and indicators assessing the effectiveness of risk management systems. In addition, there are no advance technologies of support, i.e. special control software, hardware and special communications.

The important direction for improvement of the risk management system is monitoring of the credit risk in the first place.

The practice of credit risk management in the commercial banks, especially for those with a large network of subsidiaries demonstrates that the credit committee located in subsidiaries often fail pay relevant attention to this issue. Risks in the subsidiaries exceed admissible size as a consequence, and in some cases serious disagreements arise between the head office and it subsidiaries various new banking products. Such problems happen in the presence of control system that are not efficient and appropriately organised. Subsequent closer examinations of a bank's own activities need to address such topics and when random checking is not functioning and evaluations not being performed.

Lawyers, security division, accounts department and internal audit – the bank services responsible for forecasting, averting and controlling of credit risks are often not adequately involved in the above-mentioned activities.

While forming an effective risk management system, it is problematic to make clear distinction of the authorities of the internal audit and control, and to explain their duties, stating that the latter controls the implementation of bank transactions, while internal audit prepares everything, particularly, accounting and accounting report in the run-up for the external audit.

It is also important to develop an efficient economic process in the organisation of internal controls, which in our opinion implies creation of a linear-matrix system for this purpose. The heads of the functional subdivisions or special employees are to assist internal control and audit is a part of this system.

However, organising the internal control in multi-subsidiary bank as a system is especially complicated, since there are two opposing difficulties: setting up internal control in each subsidiary is rather expensive, while the presence of the internal control only in the head office will lead to the loss of the immediate response effect on the transactions and procedures in subsidiaries; this problem will also be eliminated via linear-matrix structures.

While analysing the effectiveness of the internal control system and risk management, the following aspects must be taken into consideration:

1. Expediency of stating a risk management objective and its compliance with strategic development goals;
2. The quality of methodology for dividing risks by types, sector, clients, types of activities, limitations, budgeting aspects, plans, estimates, etc.;
3. Availability of obvious and hidden reserves for covering the

risks and achieving planned outcomes in a cost-effective manner;

4. Correctness of the risk rating determination by particular bank transactions and their total;

5. Securing the transactions with resources and monetary means;

6. Presence of the system that delegates authority to the subdivisions, especially to the an internal control service;

7. Observing requirements of legal and accounting documentation and data of the management accounts that has not adequately developed throughout and often fail to achieve modern requirements;

8. Quality of bank risk monitoring;

9. Quality of information and management systems, effectiveness of functioning of encompassing interrelations inherent in risk management.

The above-listed are the key directions of internal control while analysing the risk banking activities and it is important to consider the following essential conditions while creating a system for the management of banking risks:

1. Goal of the system – to reflect the needs of the organisation (commercial bank) at each stage so that it is protected from losses as a result of one's activities, realisation of the risks of the external environment or internal risks of the bank, and other systemic risks found in the banking system;

2. Harmonisation of interests of the bank and those of the state;

3. Resources to secure a back-up of banking risks;

4. The need to form special high level professional subdivisions within the bank.

In accordance with the goals, conditions and structural components of the system for the bank risk management are then to be defined, as it is important to identify the connection between these and functional components:

1. Diagnostic component – includes actions connected with accumulation, analysis of new data about the banking conditions needed for restructuring, about the banks that could be subject to bankruptcy and banks that are not close to such measures, an analysis of new knowledge, methods and information;

2. Forecasting actions in relation with planning the internal control activities and auditing in achieving the stated goals for the system;

3. Constructive component – actions of the bank management, as well as those of the National Bank of Georgia and other related agencies in select and building an impact system in order to influence the system of bank risk management;

4. Communicative component– includes actions to establish expedient interaction between the bank management, subdivisions under inspection and between divisions of internal control and audit. These are very important questions, and as practice has demonstrated, it has not yet been resolved by any commercial banks.

The following requirements shall be part of the the system of bank risk management:

1. Cohesiveness – implies limited number of inspections by internal control of the bank by identifying essential interconnection, sampling frames and developments.

2. Stability – implies annual, quarterly, monthly reproduction of the system of internal complex control over the bank's risks.

3. Observance – possibility to record concrete calculations, possibility to use preliminary theoretical preparation in the actual practice of commercial banks, development of special indicators of effectiveness of internal control mechanisms.

The contribution and the role of the Central Bank to the enhancement of the banking system and stability and the minimisation of banking risks are as follows: updating the legal base, and especially in connection with pressing issues, which especially applies to further improvement of the criteria for the legal base and restructuring procedures and proceeds to the financial recovery of credit institutions. The following are some of the most important issues that require immediate resolution:

1. introduction of distinct criteria, providing a complex basis for the recognition of a bank as being bankrupt;
2. establishment of a set of measures as to the responsibilities of the bank owners or the management staff concluding a deal that leads to the creditors' losses and which addresses the attributing the risks as a result of the affiliations and bank branches;
3. making use of the international experience in restructuring and it adjustment to reality;
4. further improvements in accounting and reporting standards;
5. development of a new norm document on formation of additional reserves against any potential losses of credit organisations;
6. further development of the system for complex management of bank risks, development of the relevant methods. These include methods for indicator assessment, and which indicates the presence of systemic banking risks among banking activities, analysis of exchange, interest, long-term stock market risks and the method for aggregation of all forms of bank risks.

Furthermore, with the development of the telecommunication settlement systems, the banksare able to start accommodating credits electronically with the creation of automated systems for credit and other risky transactions and under such a system it is possible to transfer to electronic format the circulation of documents between the crediting stakeholders. Such a mechanism will lead to a serious problem – as how to protect information. Many banks reject this opportunity since they have no idea as what kind of transactions and methods are applied in or enhancing the efficiency of risk management.

Further improvement of the complex system for risk management must be developed in the following directions:

1. Clear determination of strategic and operational objectives along with forecasting risks by amounts and types, stating terms, and the various means and methods of current and consecutive control.

2. Justified selection of the schemes for risk management is to be used by the bank and this can take the form of an early response in the prevention of risks, however, in such case it is important to create particularly appropriate methods. Alternatively for the bank to use a mechanism of covering the risk with relevant reserves within limitations. The optimal form of risk management will likely be a combination of forecasting methods with that of a stable reserve base one.

3. Establishing a subordination system has some options today, as there are linear-matrix systems now available, system of delegating authorities, centralised system of determination and which provide for a reduction of limits of tariffs and cost estimates. Problems emerging involve controversies between the affiliations and the bank's head office, infringement of the established risk limits for the risks, and failures in execution of budgeting plan, etc.

4. Reporting – development of the bank standards and forms for the proper management of accounts forms to track analytical internal accounting, as well as control tables, cards, matrix for budgeting and guidelines for limitations.

5. Creation of methods for management and optimisation of financial, functional, business, operational and other kinds of banking risks.

6. Development of the evaluation indicators of the efficiency of the risk management system for a number of identified errors, infringements, their subsequent impact on the results of the bank activity, status of its capital and assets, indicators of dynamic and the extent of covering risks; the facts of realising negative forecasting option of the

development of the situation on the market, and its influence on the strategy of the bank's behaviour; efficiency coefficient of the risk monitoring, as well as the measures adopted as a result of the control and analysis outcomes and in line with a number of other indicators.

In light of these considerations, it is important that each bank develop a system of complex management of banking risks and it is noteworthy that the Central Bank is able to play an important role in the formation of the risk management system within the entire banking sector. The presence of such efficient systems on the macro and micro levels will be an important step forward in averting systemic banking risks.

CHAPTER 3
Manifestations of systemic banking crises in various countries and regions

Systemic banking crises have been well documented in the era of globalisation, under such conditions economies demonstrate substantial increases in financial instability and regardless of the time and place of their origination and development, they share many common roots, such as structural weaknesses and the impact of imbalances in the banking sector. There are also various other factors involved, which may not always relate directly to sphere of banking legislation, regulation and supervision. Matters are further complicated by underdeveloped banking infrastructures, internal and external macro-economic shocks, and so forth. It is clear that taking into account the above, and including the effects of historical and national factors, it can be concluded that that any individual crisis is unique, based on many complex and interwoven interactions, based on characteristic specific to regions or countries of the world. In order to understand the nature of systemic banking crises, it is essential that we first study the diversity of processes through which they manifest themselves through the study of a number cases from throughout the world; a study to which the following chapter is dedicated.

3.1. Systemic banking crisis in the United States, 1980-1994

The US economy and banking sector worked effectively through the post-war years and did not suffer from any large-scale problems for approximately fifty years, not since the period of the Great Depression. Economic and banking stabilisers were embedded in the country's economy, particularly in the 1930s, taking the form of a scheme of deposit insurance for those with money deposits in various banks. The government and public had an active role in controlling budgetary processes and in the establishment of the Federal Reserve System, as well benefiting from favourable external economic factors that emerged as a result of the US predominance in the world's economy and standing on the political stage. All of which ensured long-term and stable economic development for the United States.

However, the systemic banking crisis that began in the US in the early 1980s, characterised by the widespread default of many savings and loan institutions brought forth havoc. A total of 1,617 banks with assets of USD 302.6 billion were either liquidated or were forced to accept financial assistance from the Federal Deposit Insurance Corporation (FDIC) to remain in business. Furthermore, 1,295 credit and savings associations with total assets of USD 621 billion were either closed down or taken under state management. The periods 1988-1992, saw the peak years of the crisis in which, on average, a bank or credit and savings institution would go bankrupt every day.

Many researchers consider that the US systemic banking crisis developed as a result of the process of liberalisation of legislation relating to lending, particularly due to the adoption of laws that deregulating the banking sector. Limitations set for interest rates on deposits and loans were eliminated, while credit and savings associations were allowed to freely enter into commercial lending markets. The change in legislation brought about a sharp increase in risk in both the credit and banking sectors, and as a result, many credit and savings institutions were not able to continue competing with traditional banking institutions that provided credit.

Later, the US monetary authorities analysed the statistics on the insolvency of banks during the systemic crisis of the 1980s, and in order to identify the causes of the crisis.

The poor quality of assets was named as the reason for 98 percent of bankruptcy cases. Poor planning, policy and management in 90 percent, abuse by insiders in 3.5 percent, the poor economic climate (35 percent), absence of effective audit and intra-bank control (25 percent), fraud and unreliable financial reporting (11 percent), and unsecured expenses (9 percent) were all identified as key factors in cases of bankruptcy.

A number of factors impacting on the quality of assets were identified, according to the Office of the Comptroller of the Currency of the US, these were: liberal terms in the provision of loans (85 percent), significant shortcomings in financial reporting mechanisms (79 percent), excessive lending (73 percent), incomplete documents used as collateral (67 percent), lending secured by goods (55 percent), excesses in the increase in the number of personnel, quantity of structural sub-units and respective expenditures (52 percent), and a large number of unsecured loans (37 percent).

A restructuring program based on the *Law on Reforms, Renewal and Law-Abidance for Enforcement of Financial Institutions* was adopted by the Congress in 1989. The law sought to overcome the crisis in the US, expanding the rights and powers of federal authorities responsible for the regulation of financial institutions. More rigorous requirements were established for the banks bringing to the forefront of the effort the enforcement of legislation, supervision and regulation. The Restructuring Trust Corporation (RTC) was established, which assumed the tasks of the asset management and liquidation of credit and savings associations. The RTC carried out the restructuring of loans held by troubled credit institutions in close cooperation with and under the control of the FDIC.

In 1991, the US Congress adopted two laws concerning the activities of the RTC and FDIC. The law on improving the effectiveness of the FDIC enabled the introduction of new levers for restructuring, namely the ability to provide immediate assistance to institutions on the verge of bankruptcy, and the power to regulate of payment settlements with creditors, with fewer incurred expenses.

The activities of the monetary authority of the US were directed towards the restructuring of problem credit institutions were remarkable due to the range of instruments utilized, as well as for the relatively effective outcomes achieved.

The process of debt resolution and the tidying-up of the affairs of failed banks in the US typically consisted of two stages: the first stage being the restructuring of the failed bank, while the second involved the liquidation of the failed bank's assets (the liquidation process), which is true in the case of any restructuring scheme, with the exception of those banks not subject to closure.

At the restructuring stage, the FDIC valued the assets of the insolvent bank, and reviewed different possible actions; the process takes into consideration a requirement for minimising the expenditure of the insurance fund. Under the circumstances were expenses were minimal, and it was possible to start the process of the acquisition of assets and liabilities of the failed bank (fully or partially) by a sound bank, the FDIC worked on a deal to wrap up the failed bank. In other cases, the FDIC ensured timely repayment to the insured depositors, and instigated the liquidation of overdue assets.

At the second stage – the liquidation process – the FDIC liquidated all remaining assets of the failed bank and distributed the proceeds first to uninsured depositors, then to the general creditors, and finally to the shareholders.

During the restructuring process FDIC continued to provide timely payment for the insured deposits. Next, at the stage of liquidation, the FDIC assumed the role of the insured depositors in the register. The entities having claims against the bank under liquidation (including the FDIC as a liquidator, bearing responsibility for administrative expenses, as well for the sum equal to the that of paid insured deposits), was paid per the order established by the *Law on General Issues of Budget Agreement* of 1993. The provisions of this agreement are known as the preferences to the internal deposits; the following order for the process is applied:

- Administrative expenses of the liquidator;
- Secured claims;
- Insured and uninsured deposits made by the US citizens (internal deposits);
- External deposits and other claims by creditors on the general list;
- Subordinated creditors claims;
- Shareholders;

The insolvency of a credit institution in the US can be defined according to the cost on the books or its market value. Accounting conventions, as a rule, bind the banks to take over the account of the assets and liabilities as based on the book value, while the *Law on Increasing Efficiency of Federal Deposit Insurance Corporation (FDICIA)* binds the regulatory bodies in the US to close down banks before they become insolvent.

The provisions of the *Law on Increasing Efficiency of Federal Deposit Insurance Corporation (FDICIA)* taking immediate corrective measures obliges the regulatory body to close down a bank if the rate of internal funds of the assets is equal to or falls below the level of 2 percent.

The rule can be justified since the market value of the bank's assets is characterised with uncertainty, and for problem banks, as a rule, it is always less than actual book cost. Winding down a bank before it becomes insolvent based on balance sheet cost, takes into account uncertainty and provides limitations to losses under the insurance fund.

In the US, the body issuing licences to the banks carrying out transactions also has the right to recall the licence as part of the expected closure of the bank.

In order to carry out deposit based banking and to attract a base of depositors, institutions in the US are required to obtain a licence.

Banking authorities at the state level issue such licences to local banks. The Office of the Comptroller of the Currency licenses the activities of the national banks, while the Supervisory Agency of Depository Institutions licences the activities of federal banks.

Following the closure of insured banks, the relevant body designates the FDIC as a liquidator. In addition, under certain circumstances FDIC has the authority allowing the wind up of a bank at its own discretion, or by excluding it from participation in the deposit insurance system. The *law on Improving the Efficiency of FDIC (FDICIA)* empowered the FDIC to start the process of bringing a bank to the position in which it will be closed, a process often completed under conditions in which a bank is considered to be seriously undercapitalised, and lacks plans for the restoration of its capital amounts to an adequate level. Furthermore, the FDIC is vested with the right to also bring a bank to closure if there is a significant decrease in assets resulting from illegal transactions where the bank carries out transactions breaching the rules without due diligence. The corresponding bank may have deliberately violated an order prohibiting the continuation of illegal actions; or the bank may have avoided the mandatory submission of data to the supervisory body. Under such conditions the bank will also lose its insured status.

The responsibilities of the FDIC under the bank restructuring process are pre-liquidation preparation of assets, their liquidation and the distribution of proceeds among the bank's creditors, less carrying charges. It should also be noted that the FDIC exercises the functions of the deposit insurer and that of liquidator at the same time. Having one agency perform both functions simplifies the procedures, avoiding duplication of records, and places the responsibility for asset liquidation on the largest creditor (FDIC), which has the incentive and capacity to obtain the maximum possible recovery of funds.

The FDIC not only has the authority to act as a liquidator, but also, based on the *Law on Efficiency Increase*, the right to designate itself as a liquidator. The above right was conferred to the FDIC in order to ensure its independence from the bodies issuing licences, and to let it act immediately to protect the insurance fund. The deposit insurer is motivated to retain the insurance fund, and under such conditions it can carry out its actions with greater efficiency as compared with the supervisory bodies that do not bear direct responsibility for the protection of the insurance fund.

The FDIC, as a liquidator, bears the responsibility for settling the affairs of the closed bank or savings institution, including collecting on its assets and, satisfying creditor claims for the proceeds. When the FDIC is appointed as a liquidator, it works as the bearer of the rights, powers, and privileges of the bank. It becomes positioned to collect all obligations and money due to the bank, manage and liquidate its assets, and perform any other banking function that is consistent with its role as a liquidator.

At the beginning of the 1980s, when the FDIC was redefining the restructuring mechanisms for failed banks, it considered a number of key issues related to how the restructuring process is carried out. The monetary authorities formulated the following principals for restructuring: maintain public trust and banking sector stability in the US; facilitate market discipline through the exclusion of transactions bearing excessive risk; carry out measures related to the failed banks in a timely and efficient manner; and act with the failed banks in an unbiased and consistent manner.

There also were some minor goals, one of which was to decrease the role of the FDIC in possessing, funding and managing the banks and their assets. After the adoption of the *Law on the Increase of FDIC Efficiency,* which specified a requirement for cost minimisation in the process of the selection of the methodology to be applied towards failed banks, the cost criteria became of greater importance than policy implementation.

Prior to the adoption of the *Law on the Increase of FDIC Efficiency,* the choice of the scheme to be applied to failed banks was different: the FDIC could carry out its work with the failed bank, applying any approach to regulate the situation that would be less costly than the repayment of deposits. The exception to this process was in those instances in which the bank was considered to be the key institution at some location in terms of servicing high quality bank services. In this case, the FDIC could apply more costly methods, above the value of deposit repayment. Cost has always been the key factor in the decision-making process in defining the methodology for working with failed banks. However, sometimes, other factors, such as the necessity to protect local populations from losses or the transfer of large assets to the liquidator, also impact on the decision-making process.

Presently, in line with the *Law on the Increase of the FDIC Efficiency*, the FDIC does not have that level of independence since it has the obligation to apply less costly methods, excluding cases that pose a "systemic risk".

Presently, the less costly approach could be replaced by another, only if two-thirds of the FDIC Board of Directors and two-thirds of the Board of Governors of Federal Reserve System are in agreement. Under these circumstances, a motion should be passed stating that adherence to cost minimisation principles should be rejected to keep the case from causing serious consequences for the economic climate or a climate of financial stability. After having made the above decision, the FRS and FDIC provide their recommendation to the US Treasury Secretary, and the Secretary having received approval from the US President, shall concur. Exclusions due to "systemic risk" have never been applied, as the *Law on the Increase of FDIC Efficiency* stipulates otherwise. However, having introduced this severe requirement, the *Law on the Increase of FDIC Efficiency* strictly specified the alternatives available for the FDIC when dealing with large banks.

There are two key methods of dealing with failed banks: financial assistance to the bank without closure, and restructuring with a view to closure. In turn, the restructuring process, leading to the future closure of the bank, can be of two types: purchase-and-assumption transactions and deposit payoffs.

From the beginning, the FDIC applied the method of providing financial assistance without bank closure when dealing with large and important banks. Under such cases, the FDIC, as a rule, would restore the capital of the bank up to the appropriate positive level through financial assistance (loan or the FDIC note), and private investors would contribute additional capital as was necessary for the bank to regain the required level of equity.

Because of the restrictions imposed by the *Law on the Increase of FDIC Efficiency*, the FDIC no longer uses the methodology of transactions without bank closure. The bank restructuring process involving future closure is generally less costly when compared to restructuring without bank closure. In the transactions with anticipated closing costs, costs are reduced because contingent liabilities are eliminated, burdensome contracts can be invalidated, and problem assets can be left in the possession of the liquidator.

Another way of working with failed banks is the creation of bridge banks that act as temporary banking institutions under the FDIC control until such time as the final decision as to how to work with the failed bank is made. In the United States, bridge banks are seldom created, though it could be expected that their establishment and operation would have some particular applications.

In the US, the function of a bridge bank would involve the transfer of assets and liabilities to the FDIC, to act as a temporary receiver and to take over the transactions of the failing bank in the interim to ensure the continuation of service provision. The FDIC Board of Directors would appoint the Chief Executive Director of the bridge bank, allowing the bank to be present before meetings of the Board of Directors.

As the name implies, the bridge bank structure is designed "to bridge the gap" between the instant bank failure and the time when the FDIC is able find an appropriate restructuring solution to the problem.

Initially, the FDIC would organise the bridge bank for a two-year period with the possibility of as many as three one-year extensions. The bridge bank would allow the FDIC to use the time to take control over the transactions of the failed bank, stabilise the situation and determine how the problem should be treated. It also enables the FDIC to have additional flexibility in dealing with the bank's restructuring.

In the US, during the banking crisis in the 1980s and the early 1990s, the monetary authorities focused on identifying methodologies for the liquidation of assets. Initially, the FDIC experts tended to manage and liquidate each asset separately. Along with the increase in asset value, under the FDIC control, the process of managing and liquidating of each separate asset base was becoming less and less practical (a loan of USD 100,000 requires almost the same service cost as a loan of USD 100,000,000). Thus, the FDIC started to gradually develop more complicated procedures for asset liquidation; among them the liquidation of a pool of assets, the creation of equity partnerships, and the securitisation of liquidated assets.

The equity partnership represents a long-term joint company, established by the Government (in the capacity of co-owner) with a private investor (in the capacity of a key investor). The government contributes a package of assets and from time-to-time, provides funding in the form of funds the working capital. The key partner brings in authorised capital and organises the audit of asset management. Initially, the equity partnerships were created and used by RTC.

Later, it was clear that managing the liquidation of each asset separately was not practical, and a change of approach was undertaken: the assets were sold in aggregate amounts – the FDIC started the formation of packages of assets with similar characteristics. However, at that time, there was not a market for such packages, and the book value of the packages ranged from USD 1 million up to USD 2.5 million.

Interest was observed in moderate packages, and the FDIC gathered information about potential buyers. Over the course of time, purchasers would gain experience and capacity and were able to attract capital and monetary resources that, in turn, served to expand their business. The book value of such packages increased gradually, and the FDIC found it possible to sell larger packages to a wider range of investors. In order to facilitate the liquidation of problem assets, the FDIC and the RTC made announcements about the quality of assets offered.

In cases in which inconsistency was found in the claimed quality of the assets, the seller was obliged to either tailor the quality to what was claimed, or to redeem or replace the asset with another one of equal value. Claims by the FDIC and RTC regarding the quality of assets ranged from the simple (the seller claims that he has rights over the credit) to more complicated ones (stipulating environmental factors).

The FDIC and the RTC applied securitization for the purpose of the liquidation of a significant portion of the assets with success. Securitization entailed grouping assets having similar characteristics and relatively predictable financial earnings, and the issue of interest bearing securities under such combined assets. In the1980s, the US the security market was backed by mortgage loans created through the Federal Corporation of Mortgage Crediting and the Federal National Mortgage Association. Thus, placing securities secured by mortgage loans on the market was much easier than placing securities secured with different assets such as, for example, commercial loans.

During the banking sector crisis in the United States in the 1980s and the early 1990s, the FDIC attracted the private sector to manage and liquidate the assets of failed institutions. During the period 1988 through 1993, the peak of crisis, the private sector managed more than 45 percent of the assets remaining after FDIC intervention. Contracts for management and liquidation of assets were worked out by the FDIC in a manner that would facilitate the liquidation of problem assets, (especially for problem loans and real estate holdings). The FDIC applied a number of different forms of agreement, were modified as more experience was gained.

Between 1980 and 1994, the FDIC sold assets to the value of USD 230.6 billion, consisting of 76 percent of total assets of the failed banks to new owners. From 1989 through 1994, the RTC took control of assets totalling USD 402.6 billion, of which 39 percent (USD 157.7 billion) were sold off at the trusteeship stage of intervention; USD 75.3 billion (19 percent) was acquired by new owners at the stage of regulation; and USD 169. 6 billion (42 percent) was left with RTC for further sale as part of the liquidation process.

The majority of researchers, evaluating the role of the FDIC and the RTC in the years of the crisis, note that the agencies succeeded in exercising timely control over the failed banks, regulating their debt liabilities, liquidating bankrupt institutions, and at the same time avoiding panic and recession in the banking sector. Their activities helped to overcome the impact of the systemic banking crisis, and to some extent, contributed to the economic revival in the US in the second half of the 1990s.

3.2 The Scandinavian model of a systemic banking crisis (Finnish case study)

Almost all Scandinavian countries turned out to be vulnerable against increasing global financial instability. The model of a social market economy that had been established in the countries of the region after World War II, gave the state a very important role in the economy. The established model of economy was characterised by high taxes, an important role for the state in the redistribution of wealth, state protectionism in industry, agriculture and other economic spheres, artificial constraints on competitiveness, which included the banking sector, and austere limitations on the credit activities of various banks.

The transition of the Scandinavian countries to a deregulated economy impacted on the banking sector in the 1980s, which when coupled with negative effect of foreign markets, led to the formation of a "Scandinavian Epidemic" and a crisis in the banking sector. There were specific catalysts in each Scandinavian country. For example, the most significant external factor in Norway was the fall in oil prices in the mid-1980s. In Finland, the collapse of the USSR acted as a trigger for a systemic banking crisis. An increase in interest rates on the international and European money markets had negative influence on almost all Scandinavian countries, and especially on Sweden.

The impact of the "Epidemic" was dramatic and significant financial resources were required to address the problem. The high concentration of capital, assets and deposits in the banking sectors of these countries also contributed to a feeling of distress across all sectors of their economies.

Compared to other countries in the region, the Finnish banking sector was under the most stringent state control before the 1980s. Constraints were in place on interest rates and other kinds of transactions related to deposits and credits in the banking sector. The issuance of deposit certificates by banks was controlled by requirements for set amounts of cash reserves. The Bank of Finland had the right to regulate the rules and credit policy procedures for its commercial banks. Credit institutions were prohibited from attracting money and resources from foreign markets. No foreign capital could be invested in the country's banking sector. The Finnish monetary policy was based on a fixed exchange rate for the national currency.

In the middle of the 80s, (1983-1986) a set of new measures was introduced in Finland, to bring about the deregulation of the country's economy, including the banking sector. The above measures were in line with the tendency towards market liberalisation prevalent in Europe at the time.

The state's complete control over the regulation of interest rates was replaced by a free choice of rates for banks on newly issued loans. Meanwhile, the limitations set on the issuance of deposit certificates were abolished, and the banks obtained the right to freely borrow on foreign markets. Branches of foreign banks appeared in the banking sector of Finland. The Bank of Finland gave up the right to directly regulate credit transactions in the period 1986-1987

The newly liberalised economy, an increase in prices for export goods and a fall in oil prices in the mid-1980s, had a short-term positive effect in terms of an economic boost, demonstrated in an increased demand for consumer goods, all types of real estate, and financial assets. The significant credit expansion of Finnish banks came with capability for substantial increases in their resource base, due to the availability of new credit and the existence of insurance for deposits and bonds. .

Furthermore, it was observed that with an increase in systemic credit risk as a result of credit expansion, coupled with the boom in the securities market, external loans taken by the Government and banks, brought about systemic currency risks. Even with bank supervision and regulation, and despite a significant increase in the risks related to banking activities, quantitative changes were not brought about. As an antidote for an excessive credit expansion, the Bank of Finland established special reserve requirements, which only led to an increase in interest rates on deposits and credits, and this action actually further increased the level of risk in the system, particularly risk related to credit, as expensive credit would eliminate many quality borrowers, and attract firms more inclined to excessive risk taking.

Thus, in the early 1990s, there were significant local macro-economic and institutional factors in Finland that formed the framework for the systemic banking crisis. However, negative external shocks in 1991 were also highly critical in bringing about the crisis.

First of all, systemic crises of the banking sector were taking place in other Scandinavian countries (Norway – 1987-1989; Sweden – 1991; with a pre-crisis situation in Denmark – 1987-1989). Finland historically had close social and economic ties these neighbouring countries and the "Epidemic" of the banking crisis, as it is referred to in the literature was one that a strong regional characteristic.

Secondly, the economy of Finland, particularly its export market, was very closely linked with the Soviet Union. A sharp deterioration in the social and economic conditions in the Soviet Union in the late 1980s led to a significant reduction of exports from Finland. The accompanying reduction in exports could not have been compensated for through the identification of other markets for export in the short run since, the competitiveness of the Finnish producers was very poor. Moreover, the problem was compounded by the crisis in the Soviet Union, as the Soviet Union was late in paying loans, and it even defaulted on some of what was owed to Finland.

The unfavourable combination of external and internal factors in Finland led to the crisis in the economy and banking sector. In 1991, the GDP of Finland fell by 2.5 percent; internal demand – by 6.5 percent, and the level of unemployment rose to 11 percent. Faced with the crisis, the fixed currency rate of the Finnish mark was reduced, and an attempt was made to level the Finnish mark with the rate of

Ecu, but these efforts were not able to prevent the devaluation that the monetary authorities were forced to implement in the autumn of 1991. Devaluation of the Finnish Mark and an increase of interest rates on the European and international financial markets further deteriorated Finland's ability to service external state debt.

The systemic banking crisis began with problem at the largest bank – Scopbank, a key player within the Finnish system of saving banks. Before the crisis, this bank was conducting an extremely aggressive credit policy. It made huge investments in Tampella Oy, and established a multi-line industrial team in order to establish a powerful conglomerate of savings banks and industrial enterprises, which was intended function as the Finnish equivalent of Korean Cheboli.

The monetary authorities worked out a programme for restructuring Scopbank, envisaging financial assistance from the State, in exchange for participation in the capital. However, the Scopbank was sharply deteriorating, liquidity-related problems started, and in 1999, the Bank of Finland took over the control of Scopbank with the aim of "retaining the trust towards the banking sector in Finland".

Along with injections of finance (more than 16 billion of Finnish Marks in total, including 9.5 billion of stabilisation credits), the restructuring scheme for Scopbank established three specialised companies that would manage the assets of the credit institution. Thus, shares under the ownership of the company were transferred to the company Scopulus Oy, industrial assets, namely the assets of Tampella, were placed under the ownership of Solidium Oy, and real estate holdings under the ownership of the bank – to Sponda Oy.

In 1991-1992, the economic crisis was accelerating with approximately 800 firms going bankrupt every month. When, the small size of this Scandinavian country is considered, such a trend proved a rather harrowing indicator. The pressure of profiteers on the rate of Finnish Mark led to the suspension of a fixed rate for the currency in autumn, 1992, which resulted in a significant devaluation.

The crisis in the Finnish banking sector grew, and in 1992, the total assets of non-operational banks amounted to 42 billion Finn Marks, of which 22 billion (5 percent of the total credit portfolio) consisted of bad credit liabilities, which were written off as losses. Almost half of the bad loans were related to real estate transactions. The drop of net interest income among Finnish banks was significant, and in tandem with a resulting fall in the quality of assets and changes in the resource base, the combined effect lead to an increase in the number of of deposits drawing high rates of interest.

In 1992, the monetary authorities of Finland began to implement a massive restructuring programme for the country's banking sector. Recapitalisation of the banking sector and the creation of an effective insurance system were the reform's main priorities.

Supervisory bodies carried out inspections of viability and evaluated the quality of the capital held by credit institutions, which allowed reliable information on this critical indicator to be obtained. Those banks, experiencing capital deficits, were provided the opportunity to benefit from recapitalisation from a pool of 8 billion Marks allocated by the government. In return, the government acquired certificates of preferred stock that was then considered as a part of its own equity, while the recapitalisation pool covered earlier losses.

In 1992, the State Guarantee Fund was established, which was granted the right to spend up to 20 billion Marks on the repayment of interest rates on deposits, and the restructuring of problem banks. Representatives of the Banks Supervisory Council, Ministry of Finance, and the Bank of Finland all participated in the management of the Fund.

Support was provided through the acquisition of shares, special certificates, and other forms of capital participation. The Guarantee Fund also had the right to issue loans, guarantees, and provide financial assistance to troubled banks. After the creation of the Guarantee Fund, the Bank of Finland transferred Scopbank to the management of the Fund for restructuring purposes and three billion Marks was spent on its recapitalisation.

The main activities of the Guarantee Fund revolved around the restructuring of the system of saving banks in Finland, which gravely suffered during the Scopbank crisis (a significant proportion of assets of the banks in the sector were held in Scopbank). A range of different approaches were applied during the process of restructuring:

Firstly, the consolidation of 41 saving banks into one single entity, the Savings Bank of Finland took place under this process.

Secondly, The State Guarantee Fund financially participated in the strengthening of the capital of the bank through the acquisition of privileged certificates to the value of 5.5 billion Marks, and guarantee against the credit on increased capital up to 1.7 billion Marks.

Thirdly, a programme to reduce the operational costs of saving banks was implemented; through a reduction in the number of branches of and the introduction of new more stringent conditions for credits and increased responsibilities for senior management.

The total cost of the restructuring programme for saving banks exceeded 13 billion Marks.

The rehabilitation of STS bank marked a significant event in the restructuring process. The State Guarantee Fund assumed the bad assets of STS totalling 3.4 billion Marks under its management.

What assets that remained were transferred to Kansallis – Osake-Pankki (KOP bank), which served the function of a bridge bank. KOP bank bore the cost of the management of STS bank, and accepted 10 percent of the losses on bad loans. The State Guarantee Fund covered the remaining 90 percent of STS's credit losses.

STS bank was operated as a "bad" bank as a result of the above-described restructuring scheme, and performed only a limited number of transactions, primarily involving the management of problem assets. Subsequently KOP bank became the owner of STS bank, and the State Guarantee Fund was granted the status of special controller with rights over the activities of STS until the completion of the restructuring process.

The total cost of restructuring the banking sector of Finland amounted to 11 percent of GDP, a much higher figure than that of Sweden (4 percent of GDP), and of Norway (8 percent).

The Finnish case study demonstrates the favourable role that an efficient deposit insurance system can play and how that process can successfully contribute to the process of systemic bank restructuring.

3.3. Systemic banking crisis as a response to tighter competition and the deregulation of an insufficiently modernised banking sector (Spanish case study)

The economy of Spain lies somewhere in the middle of the list of the most developed countries with transitional economies. This feature of the Spanish economy could be explained by a policy of state protectionism, which has been in place for many years, as well as significant market constraints that have slowed competitiveness. Only after the 1970s, as a result of political changes, the banking sector started to replace its distributive approach to the management of credit resources with a market-based policy. However, such changes proved a painful experience, resulting in the systemic banking crisis of 1978-1984.

The banking sector of Spain is characterised by a large number of factors that make it similar to countries with transitional economies. The similarity was noticeable before the crisis and continued throughout the period of restructuring in the banking sector.

Firstly, before the mid-1970s the State regulated the banking sector very closely. Applying different coefficients (investments, cash, state funds, and loans with special conditions), the state was de facto manager of the cash flow for the banks in its own interests, controlling investments aimed at modernising the industrial sector of the economy.

Secondly, the following front-line state banks played a significant role in the economy of the country: Mortgage Bank of Spain (Banco Hipotecario de Espana), Bank of Internal Loans (Banco de credito

Local), Bank of Industrial Credit (Banco de credito Industria), Bank of agricultural Credit (Banko de credito agricola), Bank of Construction Credit (Banko de credito la construccion), Bank of Foreign Economy (Banko Exterior), and National Saving Bank (Caja Postal). In many countries with transitional economies, a number of state banks still function, even being market leaders in the provision of banking services. Russia presents a very vivid example as the State Savings Bank completely dominates the banking market.

Thirdly, the economy saw a high level of concentration of banking capital, supported by the principle of "bank status quo" in accordance with the law of 1940, which prohibited the creation of new banks. It is noteworthy that the artificial concentration of banking capital occurs from time-to-time in transitional economies. In Russia, for example, the concept developed by a group of entrepreneurs led by Mr. Mamut to ensure the dominance of several dozens of large banks was considered at the state level by the Government and the Bank of Russia as the basis for the strategy of banking sector development.

Fourthly, exchange and non-banking mediators had a relatively low impact on the Spanish banking sector.

Fifthly, State protectionism in the banking sector was noticeable. The establishment of new foreign banks was prohibited until 1978. From this perspective, there are not many countries with transitional economies that are similar to Spain. Foreign capital has a dominating position in the banking sectors of many East European countries. However, a policy of state protectionism in the banking sector is practised in many post-soviet countries.

The entrance of the Spanish banking sector into major market relations, and wide-scale deregulation in the 1970s led to the manifestation of accumulated imbalances resulting in a systemic banking crisis.

The crisis of 1978-1984 began with the bankruptcy of Banca de Navarra and before its end 52 more banks would follow; almost half the banking institutions holding 20 percent of deposits were affected.

A restructuring programme was adopted with the aim of overcoming the crisis and increasing stability in the banking sector. A key component of the programme was the establishment of a deposit insurance system.

Officially, the Spanish insurance system was registered as Guarantee Funds. Each type of credit institution (stock banks, saving banks, credit cooperatives) had its own independent Guarantee Fund. The Funds were managed and operated by the State. Representatives of the Bank of Spain and the Ministry of Economy and Finance became members of the Managing Commission of the Funds.

The Guarantee Fund body has the right to manage and financially stimulate problem credit institutions with the potential for recovery, enabling them to regain solvency, in addition to the right to liquidate bankrupt institutions.

The policies towards the restructuring of problem credit institutions in Spain are rather diverse.
One of possible forms is the so-called "commercial restructuring" of the bank, meaning the merger of a problem credit institution with a solvent one. This policy was applied in the restructuring of saving banks and credit cooperatives. Merger was still considered as the most efficient and painless method of restructuring, and was usually carried out under the close supervision of the Guarantee Fund or the Bank of Spain.

The Guarantee Fund, in case of necessity, provided financial assistance to problem banks through the purchase of bad assets or the underwriting of the subordinated debt of the credit institution on preferable terms and conditions.

The above forms of restructuring would be applied under constructive positions of management of the credit institution. Otherwise, the Bank of Spain would have to take responsibility for the provisional replacement of the management bodies of the problem credit institution or assign inspectors to such institution, whose agreement would be absolutely necessary for the approval of any decision made by any management body and for it to be considered as valid.

The installation of an acting administration on the side of the Bank of Spain was also necessary in cases when "the credit institution is in an extremely difficult situation, threatening the efficiency of its own funds, stability, liquidity or solvency" or under conditions when the "actual status of the bank cannot be achieved through accounting measures". In such cases, the Bank of Spain would inform the Ministry of Economy and Finance about the measures to be carried out and publish the information in the official state bulletin.

Where "commercial restructuring" is impossible, the Bank of Spain, based on the report prepared by the management of the Guarantee Fund, proceeded to carry out the transaction – based on the so-called "accordion". Such a form of restructuring envisages the writing off of the financial losses identified by the representatives of the Bank of Spain at the expense of the capital of the problem bank. And at the same time, the owners of the bank should, after writing off the losses, retain a set level of the bank's own funds through new contributions made to the authorised capital, or subordinated credits. In such cases, it was also possible for the Guarantee Fund to purchase problem assets of the bank within the framework of the plan for financial stimulation.

The Guarantee Fund also contributed to the authorised capital of the problem bank, though, after a maximum of one year, shares under the possession of the Fund would be sold by open auction. At the same time, the buyer was obliged to meet the requirements of the Fund as required by the final financial stimulation programme for the credit institution. The fund, in the process of the implementation of the plan, could assume some other responsibilities, such as financial responsibility for the outcomes of court cases, in which the problem bank is a defendant.

If there is no way to carry out any of the above measures, the credit institution was to be liquidated under the control of the Guarantee Fund, paid off the proceeds the bank's creditors.

The Guarantee Funds actively participated in overcoming the systemic banking crisis in 1978-1984. Twenty-six banks were restructured. The transaction "accordion" was applied in case of fourteen credit institutions, seven banks were provided assistance in the form of "commercial restructuring", external management was established in three banks, repayment of insured deposits with further liquidation – in another two.

In addition, in 1983 the Government of Spain carried out compulsory restructuring of RUMASA Holding, comprised of twenty banks that had accumulated more than 5 percent of the deposits in the banking sector. The banks were transferred under the management of the Guarantee Fund with the aim of bringing about their financial reinvigoration without having to resort to the continued selling off of assets. The restructuring of these banks was carried out at the expense of the credit of the Bank of Spain, with the participation of the state and the twelve largest banks that had subscribed to the issuance of special state debt.

Along with financial stimulation of problem banks, the restructuring of the banking sector of Spain included de-nationalisation of credit institutions and the facilitation of mergers and take-overs of a number of the banks.

In the 1990s, there was considerable consolidation in the savings banking sector seeing the number of institutions reduced from 77 down to 50.

Banko de credito a la construccion was liquidated in 1982, and its funds were redistributed between Banko Hipotecario de Spana and Banko de credito Industrial. Banko de credito Industrial was also liquidated at the end of the 80s. In 1995, the assets of Banko de credito Agricola were transferred to Caja Postal and a few years earlier, in 1991 the Banking Corporation of Spain, was established for the management of the remaining state credit institutions; it was later privatised.

In summary, the restructuring of the banking sector in Spain allowed it to overcome the impacts of the systemic banking crisis and to create a competitive banking sector meeting European standards. Presently, 154 banks operate in Spain, accounting for 3.18 percent of the world's banking assets (to illustrate: the share of Austrian banks amounts to

1.32 percent, Canadian – 1.27 percent, and Portuguese – 0.72 percent). Spanish banks have strengthened since the crisis and have carried out an active expansion programme in the countries of Latin America.

3.4. Latin American banking crisis: unsustainable banking sector combined with ineffective macroeconomic policy (Argentinean case-study)

The high cost to the economy and social spending, a substantial number of inefficient programmes directed towards the restructuring of the banking sector (the most vivid examples being in Argentina and Brazil), and the intermittent re-occurrence of the crisis (in some countries there were several crises over the course of the last 20 years) are distinctive features of the systemic banking crisis in Latin America.

The banking sector of Argentina is considered to be one of the most developed in Latin America. At the same time, the characteristics of crisis in Latin America were most evident with the strongest impact in this country.

A substantial degree of imbalance and systemic risk (especially credit and currency related risk) became accumulated in the banking sector of Argentina, in the mid-1990s. The factors leading to the negative environment in the sector can be explained as follows:

Firstly, the proportion of "prime rate" credits in the credit market showed a strong downwards trend, related to the lack of competitiveness in the Argentinean banking sector, under conditions of increased demand for capital credit from foreign banks. High interest rates on loans issued by Argentinean banks scared off first-class borrowers, such as large companies, who switched to seeking foreign loans. In addition, the quality of credit portfolios was deteriorating under the burden of liabilities from bad loans, which existed in two forms: overt and disguised.

Secondly, the financial status of the state banks was deteriorating further undermined by a tendency to make decisions under pressure exerted by the authorities rather than based on their own understanding of the problems faced.

Thirdly, the banking sector could not keep pace with the sharp increase in credit risk and detect and react to it in a timely manner. Moreover, reforms of supervisory and regulatory frameworks were not implemented.

Fourthly, banking credits were increasingly shifting from the "real" sector of the economy to the financial sector.

Fifthly, the resource base of the banks was largely made up of deposits. Furthermore, unfavourable changes took place in the structure of deposits, such as a reduction in the time for deposits to mature and an increase in the share of non-residents with money on deposit.

The increase of systemic credit risk along with the rapid liberal reforms enacted by the Government of Carlos Menem favouring a fiscal policy of deregulation and dependence on foreign investors and creditors, had a significant impact on the crisis.

In the short-term, the Government of Menem was highly successful. In 1992, GDP increased by 8.4 percent, in 1993 – by 5.3 percent, and in 1994 – by 6.7 percent, this was accompanied by a unusual increase in investment. In 1994, total investments amounted to 22 percent of GDP. However, it should be noted that in most of the countries that experienced a banking crisis, the pre-crisis period is characterised by increased rates, higher than average GDP levels and total investment.

Concurrently, internal deposits in Argentina fell far below the level of those brought in by foreign investments.

Deregulation improved the capacity of the banks to give credit, and as a result their credit portfolio began to increase. However, at the same time their share of the credit compared to the "real" economy was constantly reduced from 37 percent in 1990 down to 18 percent - in 1995. The banks were becoming more and more involved in short-term profitable transactions, including the granting of credits, and profiteering from transactions within the financial sector.

There was an increase in outstanding debts and bad loans observed in the banking sector as a result. By the end of 1994, the amount of such loans totalled USD 13 billion, being about 18 percent of the total credit portfolio of Argentinean banks (it is commonly recognised that 10 percent of such loans can be considered threatening for the banking sector). It is also noteworthy that for state banks, the same indicator was 41.6 percent, for credit funds -15.5 percent, and for cooperative banks -14.7 percent.

The system of "convertibility" (tying money circulation to gold and exchange currency reserves, primarily to the US dollar), was the essence of the Government's economic policy, and such a scheme could only function with the permanent replenishment of money reserves as a result of a influx of new foreign currency. At the same time, Argentina, like the majority of developing countries, was enacting measures to artificially stimulate the positive balance of the BOP, in the Argentinean case, these measures were based on speculative capital rather than striving to maintain a positive trade balance.

Meanwhile, state expenses in foreign currency were constantly increasing, which is an example of the consequences of the Government assuming responsibility for the debt of companies undergoing privatisation, or when faced with an accumulated debt load resulting from an increase in expenses required for the servicing of external debts. Much of this was a consequence of increased interest rates on international credit markets. During the 1990s, the trade balance of the country was in deficit, and only for two years (from 1991 through 1994) the passive level of trade balance increased from USD 2.637 million to USD 4.236 million. The result was sharp increase in dependence on BOP regulation and on an influx of foreign receipts.

For three years (from 1990 through 1993) the flow of private foreign capital into Argentina increased from USD 3 million to USD 13.7 million. Eventually, the greater share of foreign investments was realised in short-term instruments - bonds with fixed interest rate that the Government and private companies offered to be traded on international financial markets. This was a noteworthy characteristic not only for the crisis in Argentina but also for Mexico, Brazil and a number of other countries as well. The downward spiral of direct foreign investments was a permanent noticeable characteristic, and in 1994, totalled only USD 1.2 million.

A rapid increase in the share of deposits in dollars was noticeable within banking structures on the eve of the crisis, and amounted to more than 50 percent of foreign currencies. Even more, 90 percent of such deposits were of short-term nature and a year or less in duration. Short-term deposits were also prevalent in the structure of deposits held in the national currency, while the share of call deposits amounted to 22 percent. Thus, along with the systemic credit risk, there was a noticeable increase of systemic risk in the liquidity equilibrium.

To compound the problem, by the end of 1994, the state budget experienced a great deficit.

The Argentinean reformers, led by Mr. Kovalio, the then Minister of the Economy, developed a programme of activities aiming at increasing the level of internal savings, promoting exports, and decreasing the passive trade balance and state budget deficit. However, the systemic banking crisis in Mexico and the devaluation of Mexican Peso undermined the trust of foreign investors and creditors in the Latino American region as a whole, including Argentina. As a result the Government was unable to implement measures intended to prevent the crisis.

The suspension of the devaluation of Argentinean Peso further aggravated the problem of the dollarisation of the economy. A panic began, overwhelming depositors who sought to withdraw their money from saving banks at once, preferring to keep their money in "stockings" or on deposit in branches of foreign banks. The deposits held in foreign banks increased by 7 percent in January 1995.

Immediately following the Mexican crisis, the effect of "hot money" emerged: financial profiteers started to withdraw money from Argentina and redirect it towards developing markets. During the first three months after the crisis in Mexico, foreign financial investments in Argentina fell by more than USD 4 billion. The total amount of deposits in the banks reduced from USD 44 billion to USD 37 billion between December 1994 and April 1995. Moreover, a significant increase of interest rates on deposits (upward of 20 percent for deposits made in Peso, and up to 11 percent - for those in USD) was not enough to bring about any tangible change in the situation. Interests rates on loans increased to rates as high as 50-80 percent. In light of such high rates, access to credit became unavailable for the real economy, even those limited credits provided by Argentinean banks became too risky, and subject to high rates of interest.

In order to overcome the crisis, the monetary authorities applied a variety of instruments, and untenably high standards for reserve requirements were reduced (from 43 percent down to 33 percent for call deposits and savings deposits, and from 3 percent down to 2 percent for deposit accounts). Later, a transition from obligatory reserve requirements to so-called "liquid requisites" was carried out. The banks of Argentina, as a result, were able to use money kept on a special account at the Central Bank. However, the banks, in exchange for the facility, took the responsibility on themselves of keeping a proportion of their assets in a certain liquid form.

The deposit on the accounts of foreign banks, state securities of member countries of the OECD, special "liquidity bills", funds transferred to the Central Bank under repo transactions, private and state bonds were included in the structure of "liquidity requisites". Thus, the crisis in Argentina, led to the optimal evolution of an instrument for monetary-credit regulation and reserve requirement enforcement.

The Central Bank, as a lender of last resort, provided financial assistance to the banks during a very acute phase of the crisis to the amount of 3 billion Pesos. In February 1995, the authorities of the Central Bank of Argentina gave additional credits to the banks undergoing restructuring. The bank had now acquired the right to provide extraordinary loans to credit institutions in amounts that exceeded their total capital. The Central Bank was allowed to purchase the credit portfolio of problem banks with the right of further sale of their portfolio to other credit institutions. Furthermore, the Central Bank was in a position to postpone the liquidation of banks by up to 120 days and introduce acting administrations in the problem banks that developed and implemented the financial recovery plan.

As the liquidation of failed banks was being carried out, during the first year of the crisis, the number of banks in Argentina fell from 163 to 123, a reduction of 25 percent.

Like in many other countries, overcoming the crisis was accompanied by the privatisation of state banks and the merger of credit institutions.

The banks working on the peripheries of the system were most likely to be subject to privatisation. Conforming with the decree of President Menem, around 51 percent of the joint stock of the above banks was transferred to the ownership of foreign banks.

The monetary authorities actively stimulated the merger process, largely through providing credit to the buyers. A fund established especially for the capitalisation of banks provided about 25 percent of the amount need for the deals associated with the sale of problem credit institutions or their credit portfolio through auction.

Enforced merger was applied with many large problem banks such as Bank Federal Argentino, Banko del Fuerte, Banko Comercial del Tandil, and Banco Cooperativo de Caseros.

Many cooperative banks were also merged and various cooperative banks were taken over by Banco Integrado Departamental (BID), the transaction costs were funded by the state.

The process of providing assistance to banks undergoing the restructuring process in Argentina, like in many other countries, involved such costs as the issuing of credits to the banks soon after those being provided assistance had faced bankruptcy, or the high cost involved in returning the problem banks to normal operations.

The status of foreign banks strengthened during the restructuring, an experience characteristic for many countries undergoing a systemic banking crisis. Foreign banks and their branches usually gain from the panic of depositors during a crisis, as they are better positioned with the opportunity to obtain significant financial resources from parent structures or partners and this allows them to acquire problem banks at a profit. It should also be noted that the Government of Spain provided direct financial assistance to foreign banks, as demonstrated with the purchase of Banco Integrado Departmental (BID) by the branches of foreign banks, such as de Boston and Banko de Galicia.

The banking capital of Spain was especially strengthened after its successful restructuring in the 1980s. This same capital was particularly active in the process of restructuring the banking sector in Argentina. Spanish banks took controlling packages of shares in three of the seven largest bank holding companies in Argentina. In 1996, the Spanish Banco Bilbao Vizcaya acquired 31 percent of the shares of a large private bank Banco Frances del Rio de la Plata. The Spanish Banco Standard bought 51 percent of the shares of Banco Rio de la Plata – the second largest private bank.

Significant changes were also noticeable in terms of banking regulation and supervision. A transition was made to the assessment of risk levels for assets and capital amounts, in line with the recommendations of the Basel Committee. The requirement that two audit companies should submit reports on the financial status of banks with capital of less than 50 million Pesos, and the anachronistic requirement for a maximum amount on saving and deposit accounts in foreign currency was abolished.

The creation of a deposit insurance system, the financial source for which was assessments to the deposit insurance fund made by credit institutions, was an important component of the restructuring of the banking sector. The amount of insurance dues for the banks was set from 0.03 percent to 0.06 percent of average monthly deposit amounts in national as well as in foreign currency. Management of the deposit insurance fund was imposed on the mixed joint company "Seguros de Depositos, S.A." (SEDESA).

The prohibition on the provision of financial support to the fund by the Central Bank and National Treasury was a significant imperfection established at the legal level. As international experience demonstrates, a deposit insurance system cannot achieve sufficient financial stability in the absence of state support, especially under the condition of unfavourable market externalities. The Association of the Banks of Argentina (ADEBA) and the Association of Foreign Banks operating in Argentina (ABRA) pointed out the above weakness in the system. Unfortunately, the internal weakness of the system was one of the reasons of for the recurrence of the systemic crisis in 2000.

The restructuring of the Argentinean banking sector received significant support from international financial institutions (IMF, IBRD, and IABD), this collective support allowed for a quick resolution to a particularly acute phase of the crisis. A significant amount of financial assistance was infused into to the banking sector. However, this decision led to an increase in foreign debt, the deterioration of BOP and an increase of state dependence on international financial institutions (and their often dogmatic proscriptions for overcoming the crisis).

In many countries in Latin America, including Argentina, the high costs related to the restructuring of the banks was not supported by conditions of efficient macro-economic policy. The deficit of the trade balance and BOP, high rate of inflation and unemployment, and outflow of capital and depositors was noticeable. Theses countries, succeeded in overcoming the results of the systemic crisis in spite of the challenges faced. However, still they failed to establish a stable economy and the kind of vital banking sector that would have been a strong bulkhead against negative externalities.

The main lesson learned as a result of the systemic crisis and restructuring of the banking sector in the Latin America is that without built-in stabilisers and the existence of realistic macro-economic policy and above all a reliance own internal capacity, no restructuring with long-term positive results can be achieved.

3.5. South-East Asia under systemic crisis in the banking sector (South Korean case study)

The systemic banking crisis in the countries of South-East Asia was the most significant demonstration of global financial instability, as well as an indicator of the inefficiencies in the policy of international financial institutions that operate in the economic and banking sectors of developing countries.

The systemic banking crisis in these countries began in 1998. The swiftness of its development (the so called "contagious pattern"), and the scale of the damage that was felt by the economies of the region can only be compared with the last "epidemic" in Latin America. The damage done to Indonesia totalled 50-55 percent of its GDP; in Malaysia – 21 percent; in the Philippines – 7 percent, in Taiwan – 11.5 percent; and in Thailand – 42 percent of its GDP. It should also be noted that the destructive effects of the crisis have still not been overcome to date.

Many prominent politicians and experts on systemic crisis focus their attention on the crisis in South East Asia in their speeches and research.

According to Mr. J.M. Severino, the Vice-President of Asian Department at the World Bank, the systemic banking crisis in South-East Asia predicts the nature crises in the 21st century, and was the result of a combination of the following factors: the excessively high rate of debt of the countries of South-East Asia, the rapid opening of their national economies to foreign investment.

Mr. P. Walker, an American expert, the Head of Federal Reserve System of the US between 1979-1987, noted that the loss of trust in depositors by investors, including foreign investors, in addition to the nature of the financial and banking systems of the affected countries is what brought about a rapid outflow of deposits and capital, the main reason for the crisis.

Mr. Krugman, a well-known expert on systemic banking crises, professor at the Massachusetts Institute of Technology (MIT), noted that corruption and nepotism developed on a massive scale, and large amount of credits were given to the firms involved in profiteering transactions in the real estate markets, while at the same time banks and other financial institutions ignored the level of credit and market risk, which ultimately resulted in the creation of a "financial bubble" that would inevitably burst.

In the example of Korea, we can well observe not only the genesis of the banking crisis but also the successful implementation of a programme for the restructuring of the banking system.

The crisis in Korea reached its peak in late 1997 when the transactions of 18 of the 34 registered banks (16 were later liquidated) were suspended.

The Government of Korea developed a programme directed towards the restructuring of the banking system consisting of the following principles:

- The banking system should be restructured rapidly and completely with the aim of the swift reactivation of the key function of the financial mediator;
- Budget expenditures for restructuring should be under strict control and regulation;
- State support should only be rendered to those banks that sharply reduce current expenses and attract foreign investments for recapitalisation;
- All activities within the framework of restructuring should be transparent to avoid future litigation.

After the licences of some banks were revoked, the Government started the process of restructuring problem credit institutions.

The greatest problems were noticeable in major backbone banks, such as Korea First Bank and Seoul Bank. The shareholders were required to cover the losses of the banks through charging-off their shares to the authorised capital. The authorised capital of these banks was written off by more than 80 percent, up to USD 100 million. After having accomplished this, the state nationalised these banks and proceeded to recapitalising them. The capital of the banks was increased up to USD 1.25 billion (1.5 trillion won) at the expense of the Government's resources.

At the recommendation of the International Monetary Fund, programmes of privatisation were implemented in the recapitalised banks.

A Government decree was issued for the remainder of the banks, requiring the submission of plans for their recovery noting sources of capital replenishment within the following six months.

Leading western consultancies and audit companies actively participated in the process of restructuring Korean banks. For example, Merrill Lynch, a foreign entity put USD 400 million into the capital of Kookmin Bank; Chase Securities invested USD 250 million into Industrial Bank and Paine Webber, infused USD 250 million into Korea Development Bank.

The Government Commission, established as a response to the crisis, decided to affiliate the five restructured banks with sound banks, having a sufficiency coefficient of capital no less than 9 percent; these banks were then inspected by international audit companies. In order to redeem the problem assets of banks under restructuring, a special organisation – Korean Assets management Corporation (KAMCO) - was established.

Furthermore, the banks least affected by the crisis, were ordered to increase their own equity, change top management, and make improvements in their balance of currencies and volume of transactions.

About 75 percent of the authorised capital of the Korean banking system passed to the state during the restructuring process. Later, the state sold the majority of its share holdings to foreign investors.

The Korean experience (in which the economy lost approximately 20 percent of GDP) demonstrates that rapid and efficient measures taken by the authority can successfully overcome the results of destructive systemic banking crisis.

3.6. Systemic banking crisis in transitional economies (Bulgarian example)

The vast majority of developing countries proved vulnerable in the face of systemic banking crisis. Decentralisation and privatisation in the economy, including the banking sector, were often not accompanied by the adequate and timely establishment of necessary legislative controls and appropriate financial institutions.

Commercial banks in many countries with transitional economies started their operations several years prior to the adoption of basic legislation such as Laws on Banks and Banking Activities or Laws on Central Banks. Such institutions were established on an emergency basis and often served as nothing more than décor rather than as efficient instruments of a market economy, as large, enduring historical divides continued to exist in the spheres of economic, cultural, legal and moral traditions.

Transition countries mostly depended on the openness of their economies to foreign investment for financial growth, which largely did not lead to a significant increase in capital investments into the modernisation of national economies, but rather made their financial and currency markets most attractive for the kind of transactions more related to profiteering. Structural imbalances in economies, distorted budgetary policy, inefficient management of balance of payments, trade balance and money circulation created the basis for economic and currency crises in the countries with transitional economies.

The insufficient capitalisation of banks, inefficient risk management, the absence of institutions necessary for the resolution of problems related to information asymmetry, and the deficit in systems for the protection of creditors' interests made the banking systems of these countries vulnerable in the face of negative externalities and internal weaknesses.

Consequently, taken together, amongst such countries, a complicated symbiosis of socio-economic, currency and systemic banking crises began. The data about the damage to a number of economies demonstrates the scale of the crises. For example, the damage inflicted on the Czech Republic totalled 12 percent of GDP; in Hungary – 10 percent; in Macedonia – 32 percent; in Russia – 5-7 percent, and in Slovakia – 15 percent of GDP. Along with this, in some countries with transitional economies systemic banking crises or so-called "borderline conditions" were repeatedly observed.

Restructuring for the above countries was, as a rule, a long process, quite often leading to significant strengthening of foreign capital (Poland, Czech Republic, Hungary, and other countries). During the restructuring process, deposit insurance systems and credit bureaus were established in the majority these countries and tangible results were noted in the improvement of the quality of the banking supervision and regulatory oversight. However, the banking systems of these countries were not able to accumulate sufficient stability reserves that protect against banking crises. Furthermore, the possibility of the development and recurrence of such crises in the near future cannot be completely excluded.

In the example of Bulgaria, we can see the reasons, processes and means to overcome a systemic banking crisis in a transitional economy.

In the late 1980s, the process of transition from a centralised economy to a market economy began in Bulgaria. Like in many other countries with transitional economies, special line banks emerged in the country, and over a short period of time these were transformed into joint-stock banks. In the early 1990s, a significant amount of bad debt from insolvent enterprises within the state sector of the economy accumulated on the balance sheets of these banks. Later, the Government registered the debt as long-term public bonds. However, the People's Bank of Bulgaria, due to unmet liabilities taken by the Government, had to recognise their public bonds as questionable assets, for which the banks had to create appropriate reserves as a hedge.

The increase in the number of commercial banking institutions in

Bulgaria in the early 1990s was accompanied by a significant expansion in credit. Simultaneously, the quality of risk management, primarily with regard to the quality of credit, did not match the level of risk whatsoever.

Based on data provided by the supervising bodies in 1996, the total loan portfolio of the banking sector in Bulgaria amounted to 924 billion Levis (USD 12 billion), its quality was characterised through the following indicators: standard loan indebtedness – 51.31 percent; doubtful loans – 33.26 percent, and bad loans – 16.43 percent. Thus, the level of bad loan arrears exceeded the critical level accepted by international financial institutions – by as much as 10 percent.

Another indicator of systemic loan risk - the ratio of large credits to capital – was also extremely high. In 1996, the sum of large loans in the banking system exceeded capital by 1089 times, while the maximum allowable level, based on international standards, as well as on local legislation was 800 percent. The above figures, testify to the poor quality of banking regulation and supervision in Bulgaria.

The consequent damage brought about by the loss of credits, first of all, led to a rapid fall in funds in Bulgarian banks. In 1995, the total capital of the banking sector of Bulgaria dropped from 16 billion Levis down to 10.5 billion, i.e. by one-third (34%), and its ratio to the sum of assets, weighted, and considering risk, amounted to a reduction of 1.3 percent by the beginning of 1996, at the time the minimal admissible level was considered to be 8 percent.

As a result, the ratio of bad loans to the total capital of the banking sector amounted to 214 percent in 1997. Thus, the banking system of Bulgaria actually had a deficit on its own funds, not subject to replenishment through any ordinary methods.

Alongside the extremely high indicators of systemic credit risk and the risk of capital insufficiency, the systemic risk of imbalanced liquidity was also growing rapidly. Many banks stopped providing current banking services to their clients. The panic among private depositors eager to withdraw their deposits could be observed in the socio-political situation in the country that increasingly deteriorated with the problems of the banking sector.

Structural imbalances in the banking sector of Bulgaria in the mid-1990s were further negatively affected by unfavourable macro-economic and institutional factors.

A chronic budget deficit was observed in Bulgaria in the 1990s that destabilised the macro-economy of the country. Bulgaria experienced hyperinflation and a deep drop in production capacity. Furthermore, Bulgaria had significant foreign debt. For example, in 1996 the payments made to cover foreign debt amounted to more than USD 1 billion, which led to an increased imbalance in public finances and the unexpected necessity for the Government to request funds from the People's Bank of Bulgaria.

Under the conditions of hyperinflation, the rates from the Central Bank for re-financing rose to 72 percent, while the rates for credit banks increased up to an even greater level. This created conditions which drove first-class borrowers out of the market and further aggravated excessive credit risk.

Unable to avert the increased instability in the banking sector, the regulatory bodies demonstrated complete inefficiency. The problem of information asymmetry was also very vivid.

The rise of negative macro-economic and institutional challenges, as well as structural inequalities in the banking sector, were further complicated by the currency crisis in 1995, which in turn led to a systemic banking crisis damaging the national economy and reducing GDP by 13 percent.

In order to overcome the consequences of the crisis of 1996-1997, a restructuring program for the banking system was developed by the IMF and WB and successfully implemented by the Government of Bulgaria.

The goal of the programme was macro-economic stability based on the recovery of public finances and the establishment of an enhanced monetary and credit policy at the People's Bank of Bulgaria. As a result of these activities, macro-economic conditions stabilised; inflation, the rate of re-financing, and interest rates were reduced making it possible to provide credit to the "real" sector of the economy.

Significant changes were also implemented in the *Law on Banks and Banking Activities*. These changes now made it possible to establish a legal basis for the Central Bank's regulatory activities. The authority of the People's Bank of Bulgaria was increased in the sphere of aid to problem banks, as well as granting the ability to revoke the licences of and initiate bankruptcy proceedings against failed banks.

In 1996, a state deposit insurance system was put into operation in Bulgaria, envisaging 100 percent insurance for deposits made by individuals and privatisations funds, and 50 percent insurance for those made by legal bodies (except for financial institutions). Establishment of a Deposit Insurance System facilitated the restoration of public trust in the banking sector and stabilised the reserve base of the credit institutions.

Within the framework of the restructuring programme, recapitalisation of state banks was implemented with the goal of further privatisation. Agreements were made on special modes of management under the control of international financial institutions as a provisional stopgap measure prior to the eventual privatisation of such banks.

The banking sector of Bulgaria adopted international stocktaking, accounting, audit, and supervision standards. Basel standards for the assessment of capital and risks were also introduced.

During the process of the restructuring of the corporate and banking sectors, the introduction of European socio-economic standards (linked to EU accession) enabled Bulgaria not only to overcome the consequences of systemic crisis, but also to bring about a transition to a new, modern and stable banking system.

CHAPTER 4

Role of banking regulation and supervision in overcoming systemic banking crises and creating sustainable banking system

Systemic banking crises in both developed and developing countries exposed issues of inadequate banking supervision and regulation that exist at the on-set of the crisis on the level of systemic banking risks and their impact. In addition, the experience of a number of countries (Denmark, the Netherlands, Great Britain, etc) convincingly demonstrates that an efficient system of banking supervision and regulation plays a crucial role in averting systemic banking crises.

In recent years, the system of the banking regulation and supervision, both at the national and international levels, has undergone dramatic changes. In the past decade, the supervisory authorities have started to closely regulate the risks which had not been previously clearly defined. These are considered as key indicators used in assessing the sustainability of both individual credit institutions as well as the banking system as a whole.

4.1. Regulation of capital adequacy

Capital adequacy was considered by supervisory authorities as the key element in order to achieving stability within the banking system. Long and heated discussions in determining the optimal degree of supervision were held among representatives of the banking community. As a result, the much discussed and widely recognised Basel agreements on capital and risk assessments of the credit institutions appeared in the forefront.

In carry on this discussion, an understanding of capital adequacy and its two aspects in the international practice is required: institutional and that of capital-risks ratio.

The institutional aspect implies that each bank as an institutional setting, and properly licensed body, must maintain an acceptable minimum level of authorised or equity capital. In the majority of the developed countries, the norm of institutional capital adequacy is fixed at 5 million Euros (or an amount in the national currency equivalent to 5 million Euros). In addition, non-bank credit institutions can also carry out their activities alongside of banks for which this norm is established, but a rule, at a significantly lower standard.

The application of the norm of the institutional capital adequacy is a subject of frequent heated discussions and especially among the countries with developing economies. Opponents of this standard often highlight the priority need to assess the capital adequacy in relationship with risks. Furthermore, mechanical introduction of such a high standard in regard to the equity capital in the countries where the banking system is still in the process of formation could, as many of it opponents consider, lead restrictions of competition and discuss how that would in turn negatively impact the sustainability of the banking sector. Further, it is also thought that both aspects of capital adequacy – institutional norms and the norms that are based on the comparison of the equity capital and risks – must be taken into consideration.

At the present time the capital adequacy that has been incorporated into the banking laws of the majority of the countries operates as a ratio of the amount of the equity capital and risks as a determining indicator of being able to demonstrate the sustainability of a credit institution.

In 1988, the Basel Committee on Banking Regulation and Supervision adopted the document "International Convergence of Capital Measurement and Capital Standards" hereafter, the so called the Basel Agreement) that established the method of calculating the norm of capital

Efforts made by supervisory authorities among developed countries in determining the optimal size of the capital adequacy has been clearly defined by Wayne D. Angel, a member of the Federal Reserve System board of directors: "It is difficult to state the exact figure, but I assume that the minimum capital of the banks shall comprise of approximately 10 percent of the weighted risk assets. If 10 percent seems too high of a limit, it should be noted that before the introduction of the deposit insurance system, the share of equity capital usually exceeded 20 percent. Moreover, in those fields of financial service where deposit insurance system does not exist, the relative weight of the equity capital was significantly higher than 10 percent. However, to mitigate the difficulties of the transitional period, increase in the relative weight of the own banking capital will take a lot of time."

It depends on the actual value of this coefficient, as supervisory authorities were defining the integral financial status of the bank, and the failure to achieve this norm is considered in the legislation of the majority of the countries as an indication of bankruptcy. Such a status is associated with many consequences. Within the methodology, as developed by the Basel Committee, and later subsequently adopted by virtually all developed and the majority of developing countries, capital constituents are divided into two levels or groups.

The first level capital includes permanent stock capital, i.e. issued and completely paid ordinary stocks and interest-bearing preferred stocks and those without cumulative payment of dividends, recorded reserves, additional paid-up capital, undistributed profit, general reserve and how these cover incidental (windfall) losses and other reserves funds established by banks in compliance with acting national legislation. The process also incorporates investments in the affiliated enterprises that are not necessarily part of the consolidated balance sheet of the bank (minority interests).

The second level capital includes other types of reserves, particularly hidden reserves and the reserves used in conducting a reassessment of assets.

Depending on the national banking legislation, these components are differently applied in practice. For example, the law of many countries prohibits inclusion of the hidden reserves not recorded in the balance sheet of the bank in the calculation of the capital adequacy, though they could be quite sound monetary funds and they could be applied as protection against risks; whereas, the Basel Agreement envisages the possibility of using them as a capital on the second level.

Another component of the additional capital – the reserves for the assets reassessment – is formed when the assets value is recalculated based on current pricing terms, while the balance sheets would reflect their initial value (buildings, securities, etc.). For example, while calculating capital coefficient, the Agreement allows for nominal profit from the reassessment of the securities with a significant discount (no more than 45 percent of the growth of the portfolio value is permissible) to be taken into consideration.

The next component for the second level of capital – general reserve for potential losses on loans – is included, and only if it serves as coverage for contingent losses from the loan portfolio. If this reserve is assigned to cover the losses of already identified unsound loans, it cannot be freely used for the reimbursement of contingent losses and respectively, could not be incorporated in the capital calculation.

And finally, some types of securities combine the features of stocks and debt liabilities (preferential stocks with cumulative dividend, bonds, compulsory convertible into stocks, etc) could these are also included in the second level capital.

Another type of the liabilities issued by banks and that has recently acquired special popularity in the west also plays an important role.

These are so called subordinated bonds – a special type of securities not backed up by special collateral and subject to repayment in case of bankruptcy of a bank after the creditors' claims are met. To be included into capital, it is necessary that primary maturity date of such bonds be no less than 5 years, and the amount to be calculated not to exceed 50 percent of the value of first level capital. Subordinated borrowings could also be mobilised in the form of credits and not as bonds.

The total amount of the capital of the first and second levels forms a numerator of the calculation formula of the capital adequacy coefficient. The denominator of this formula is a sum of banking assets weighted in terms of the degree of risk, other risks (on extra-balance sheet operations, interest, stock, and exchange derivatives) minus reserves.

Risk assessment of extra-budgetary transactions is a rather complicated process. It is well-known that the banks usually record conventional and guarantee transactions on the balance sheet. At such time as responsibility of the bank is faced with probable issues, the Agreement envisaged the following risk assessment procedure on these transactions be carried out. At first nominal amount of extra-budgetary obligations is transferred into the equivalents of the credit risk and then, the obtained amount is weighted in compliance with the category of the borrower as recorded in the balance sheet operations.

The introduction of the banking supervision of the assessment of the sustainability of the credit institutions by means of norms of the capital adequacy has brought forth certain fruits, such as the average indicator of the capital adequacy of the credit institutions of the developed countries having increased from 9.3 to 11.2 percent in the past decade. However, the ever increasing globalisation of the financial relations and associated banking has made it necessary to search for new ways to assess the sustainability of credit institutions, which includes new methods of risk and capital adequacy assessment.

In 1999, the Federal Reserve System and Foreign Exchange Control Agency of the US issued directives on banking operations risk management. Key elements of credit risk management were reviewed in the document and focused on the idiosyncrasies of concrete types of counteragents and organisation of permanent collection and an analysis of the information about the counteragent. The information shall be as detail as possible and reflect a particular risk. In regard to security, the FRS warns against the overestimation of its importance and underlines that even in case of using security it is necessary to carry out clear policy to define the possibility of losses and determine the size of the additional reserves, as well as to observe provisions of the agreement. .

The efficient assessment system of credit risks must provide sufficient information in order for the bank to be able to take special measures in controlling risks, as necessary. In addition, these systems shall be based on the realistic analysis of potential risks, and need to apply testing and scenario analysis of the potential development. While conducting such analysis, it is important to further consider the impact of the market volatility on the risks of the individual counteragents, as well as the impact of changes of the market liquidity on the assessment of the above-line accounts.

Aggressive testing (including the assessment of the bank behaviour in case of the worst scenarios, changes in the market liquidity and unique characteristics of the credit portfolio) will assist the managers in assessing the maximum losses that the credit portfolio could incur. Alternatively, the traditional methods used are unable to to assess the changes of yield under risk or price risk. It is important to pay attention to such special operations as unconfirmed deals with securities that include preliminary agreement on main conditions and internal assessment of low liquid securities.

Taking into account the negative experience of operations with hedge funds, supervisory authorities in the US recommended that banks possess complete financial information from all counteragents, including balance sheet and additional balance sheet accounts, details of the current policy and current operations, complete quantitative assessment of the concentration and the level of risk, as well as the information about the liabilities of the borrower in terms its other creditors.

Moreover, the bank is also required to inspect the efficiency of the credit risk management systems as used by its counteragents. Testing of the capability to overcome the faced difficulties or even when faced with incredible situations is necessary in revealing particular counteragents or the groups more vulnerable to intense changes in the market situation and to further examine the price risk management systems. Reviewing the proposals made by hedge funds, the bank has to assess their compliance with not only the client's needs but also with acting legislation and the regulations..

Along with the initiation of the national supervisory authorities, the new risk and capital adequacy assessment methods were proposed at the international level. In June 1999, the report of the Basel Committee was published and this document contained the new approaches to the problem of ensuring capital adequacy and improvement of the control over the banks to observe enforced norm of regulation and described how these were formulated.

The most important difference of the new control scheme from the principles of the Agreement of 1988 is that it is based on more substantial foundation – three parallel functioning pillars as they are called in the report or operational components:

- Minimum capital requirement;
- Intense control by the supervisory authorities over compliance with these norms;
- Compliance with market tenets.

The Committee offered to extend the composition of accountable risks. Three large categories have been identified: credit risk (especially the risk connected with the loan portfolio), market risk and other types of risks (firstly, operational risk and interest risk in terms of the accounts of the bank's balance sheet, as well as the risk of liquidity loss, deterioration of reputation, etc). The methodology for identifying and qualifying the third category of risks is not sufficiently developed yet and the work on them still continues.

To improve the accuracy of the risk assessment connected with various categories of the assets, it was offered to provide the banks with the possibility to use external credit ratings published by specialised financial agents, professionally conducting the assessment of investment availability of financial instruments, as well as the ratings of the insurance companies that guarantee export operations. Standard and Poor's, Moody's service, Fitch IBCA are the most eminent companies in this field.

The new methodology has defined the borrower's following key categories: high authority (central government and the central bank of the country), commercial banks and non-financial companies of the real sector. This method allows application of new weighing assessments of risks – and in particular, more than 100 percent (for example, 150 percent). Furthermore, it was offered for the method to be used liquidate current division of borrowers among the member states of OECD and the countries outside of this group as well.

As the practice proved such a division does not correctly reflects the quality of demands to the relevant clients of the bank since the countries of OECD are not homogenous. Furthermore, according to the new method the risk coefficient assigned to the borrower within each category depends on the external assessment of the relevant debt liabilities by the reputable credit agencies. For example, if the public debt of the country has the highest rating (from AAA to AA – classification of Standart and Poor's), zero coefficient of risk is assigned to the claims; in case of the rating from A+ to A-, the risk comprises 20 percent, from BBB+ to BBB- - 50 percent, etc. If the rating of the public debt of the country is below B-, it is assigned 100 percent of risk when the adequacy of the banking capital is calculated.

There is a possibility to reduce the risk coefficient (increase the rating) for the public debt for the countries that submit complete information about the situation of its economy and finances in terms of the IMF programme on the standards of the information dissemination based on the new provisions.

In the second group (banks), the determination of the potential risks has also changed. Two alternative approaches are envisaged: on the basis of rating of indebtedness of high authority of the country where the bank is located and on the basis of individual assessment of the bank liabilities by the external rating agency. In the first case the risk of demands to the banks is by one gradation higher than the risk of demands to high authority (for example, 50 percent against 20 percent). In the second case the risk coefficient, as a rule, equals 50 percent. However, if the bank has highest rating, the risk declines to 20 percent and in case of low rating goes up to 100 percent.

In the third group (non-financial companies) the risk coefficient is maintained at the level of 100 percent. But if the liabilities of the company have highest rating, the risk could be as low as 20 percent and in case of rather low rating, which could be increased to a level of 150 percent.

The requirements towards non-central public sector entities have the same risk coefficient as the demands to the banks of this country, but by the decision of the supervisory authorities this assessment could be increased (risk reduced) to the rating of indebtedness of the high authority. The similar scheme is applied to the broker companies.

In terms of off-balance sheet assets, the current assessment method that includes a conversion factor is retained. The liabilities of the bank on extending credits (credit lines, etc.) up to one year which are assigned a zero indicator of risk being the exception.

German experts evaluated new rules suggested by the Basel Committee and determined that they will lead to the growth of capital adequacy norm for the large banks of the developed countries by 6-14 percent that could account for higher interest rates on provided credits.

Since specialised rating agencies play a crucial role in the new system, the order of selection of these instruments is clearly outlined on the basis of a number of criteria (objective and with the use of unambiguous methods, independence from the political influence, confidence by rating agencies, and the transparency of assessment, etc).

It can be assumed that it will not be an easy task for those countries in transition, and others not having at this time very developed banking infrastructure (absence of internationally recognised rating agencies) to make a transformation to risk assessment methodology.

The realistic assessment of the capital adequacy of any bank is also complicated by the fact that these countries have not yet been completely accepted international financial reporting standards (IFRS) in actual practice. Experts consider that the transition of the banking sector of these countries to IFRS will reveal the inadequacy of capitalisation of many banks and weaknesses in their economies. Moreover, considering the general instability of the economic situation in countries, as well as potential threats of systemic banking crises, the transition to IFRS during the assessment of the capital adequacy and other indicators of bank stability should be of an evolutionary character and should be accompanied by added measures of amortisation.

Therefore, the capital adequacy indicator is an integrated indicator of the assessment of the sustainability of the credit institution, since capital adequacy is used to calculate virtually all types of risks of the banking activities. Concurrently, the type of risks now face have a tendency of being diverse and the banking community faces the need to constantly upgrade methods risk assessment on a regular basis. Furthermore, to resolve this objective coordination of the efforts of supervisory authorities, as well as of the banks, consulting companies, rating agencies and the participation of the academic community is essential.

4.2. Regulation of liquidity of credit institutions

Banking crises that have become more and more frequent are connected with the limitless transfer of what is best described as speculative capital and such transfers are made in an environment of deregulation within national financial markets, instability of currency exchange markets, securities market and this happens in a combination effort with accrued liabilities, which is the reverse side of the globalisation in international financial system. Therefore, the maintenance of the required level of liquidity alongside of capital adequacy of credit institutions, as well as regulation of other risks of the credit institutions, is a permanent objective that merits the continued attention of national supervisory authorities.

Internationalisation of the monetary markets leads to the increase of the risks of the credit institutions, which includes liquidity loss risks that brings about pressure to devalue various types of assets. Oftentimes the assets tend to devaluate as a result of fluctuation in exchange rates. This happened in South-East Asia in 1997, in Russia – in 1998, in Georgia – late 1998 and early 1999, and in Turkey, in 2001.

Furthermore, crises are not restricted to only the sphere of money circulation and they often provide the conditions that lead to origins of acute instability on national stock markets, and these are involved with fluctuation in rate that securities are traded.

Such events are responsible for panic among the investors and uncontrollable avalanche-like outflow of capitals from the country, thus creating additional problems to already stressed credit institutions and central banks having to deal with issues of liquidity management. These problems become even more complicated with dealing with the root causes of the liquidity crisis, and the banking system faces problems when the credit institutions have to meet one's liabilities in covering fixed-term contracts at a time when base assets of the futures contracts are continuing to devalue.

The behaviour of the Central Bank is very important when dealing with efforts to avert the crisis in the banking system and this is often done along with the efforts of credit institutions, and the . following measures are to be applied under such circumstances.

- change (mitigation) of the regulatory rules of the prudential supervision;
- extending credits to credit institutions;
- change of the monetary and credit policy.

To regulate liquidity of the credit institutions, the central banks can also apply special directive coefficients, as well as analysis of the indicators that are of an advisory character. Both directive and advisory indicators are different, and depending on the type of the credit institution, and how the Central Bank evaluates the implementation of these coefficients, there are varying degrees of impact, especially direct impact on the bank, and this necessary in face of challenges.

Central banks in many instances control the total transformation of money flows in the both national and foreign currencies, and even in some cases, they consider it as expedient to divide up these flows. A similar trend is observed in terms of geographic consolidation. Furthermore, inter-banking assets and liabilities tend to be more frequently united in liquidity management practice. Central banks have been trying timely to bring about the analysis of the liquidity status of credit institutions and take preventive measures to avert the systemic banking crisis in real time.

Using the example of central banks of a few countries, we shall review sensible norms and practices of liquidity management of various credit institutions.

In the banking practice world-wide, various approaches for the assessment of the solvency and liquidity of a bank are applied.

The bank of France, for example, assigns the French commercial banks to observe short-term and medium-term liquidity ratios.

The short-term liquidity ratio (R stl) is calculated by means of the following formula:

$$R \; stl = \frac{LF}{F+M} \times 100\%$$

where LF - is liquid funds on assets;
F - funds on demand on liabilities;
M – difference between mobilised and allocated bank deposits for the term of three months.

Short-term liquidity ratio is correlation of liquid funds on assets and funds on demand on liabilities.

The Bank of France considers as cash in hand current accounts in the central and other banks, bills of to three-month maturity, extended credits subject to rediscounting in the official organisations, export credits secured by COFACE (Foreign Trade Insurance Company of France) etc.

Current accounts, cash vouchers, rediscounting of bills to three-month maturity, savings accounts belong to the funds on demand, as well as the difference between mobilised and allocated banking deposits for the term of up to three months.

Minimum norm is 60 percent. Accountability on short-term liquidity ratio is submitted once a quarter.

Medium-term liquidity ratio looks as follows:

$$R \ mtl = \frac{R}{AF} \times 100\%$$

where, R - is resources for the term of two years,
AF - funds allocated for the term of longer than two years.

Medium-term liquidity ratio is correlation between resources for the term of more than two years (equity capital, savings accounts, obtained credits, deposits, credit lines 'stand-by') and the resources, allocated for the term of more than two years (not subject to rediscounting in the official organisations, deposits). The minimum norm is 80 percent. Accountability on this indicator is submitted to the Bank of France once a quarter.

Furthermore, the Bank of France makes estimates on the liquidity for the coming year on the basis of the analysis of incoming and outgoing money flows.

In Germany, whose experience is worth to mention, the functions of regulation of the commercial banks' activities are assigned to the Bundesbank and Federal Credit Control Agency. Bundesbank has only one real means to affect the activities of the credit institutions – to set minimum rates for inspection. In addition, Bundesbank receives the accounts of the credit institutions; however, the supervision is conducted directly by the Federal Credit Control Agency.

Working in close relations with the Bundesbank, the Federal Credit Control Agency is liable to watch that the provisions of the law on credit activities be observed, react to the infringement and ensure the currency stability. This federal agency acts on behalf of particular banks and the economy of the country on the whole.

In Germany the accounts on the status of the balance sheet liquidity of the bank is submitted to the Bundesbnak at the end of each month in terms of the following formula:

Formula 'A'.
Assets (A1): the claims to the banks and non-banks for four-year and more term + unquoted securities + participation + fixed assets.

Liabilities (L1): equity capital + liabilities to the bank and non-bank organisations for the term of four years and more + 10% of liabilities to non-bank organisations for the term of 4 years + 60% of saving deposits+60% of assignments to the pension reserve.

Correlation of assets (A1) and liabilities (L1) shall not exceed 100 percent.

Formula 'B'.

Assets (A2): 10 percent claims to the banks for the term from three months to four years +claims to non-bank organisations for the term of four years + purchased 'a'forfe' bills + other assets after the value of gold and other precious metals.

Liabilities (L2): 10% liabilities to the banks for the term to three months + 50% of liabilities to the banks for the term from three months to 4 years + 20% of saving deposits+60% of liabilities to non-bank organisations for the term to 4 years (excluding deposits) + assets of the formula 'A' (A1) after liabilities (L1).

Correlation of assets (A2) and liabilities (L2) shall not exceed 100 percent.

Formula 'C'.

Assets (A3): claims to the companies, private persons and foreign state organisations + bill credits to the companies, private persons and foreign state organisations + 50% of claims and bill credits to foreign banks, as well as probable claims on guarantees to the local companies, private banks and non-bank organisations + 20% of claims and bill credits, as well as probable claims on guarantees to the banks of the Federal Republic of Germany.

Liabilities (L3): equity capital.

The allocated resources in the bank calculated by this formula shall not exceed 18 multiple size of its equity capital.

In the USA supervisory authorities of assessment of reliability and liquidity of banks apply the CAMEL system which is based on the assessment and analysis of the activities of banks methodology developed by the experts of the American bank Sheshunoff Bank.

Each assessment criterion group is essential for the analysis, but the specialists of the bank pin special importance to the factors of the bank reliability, presence of problem credits, income sources and large liabilities of the bank.

The methodology of the assessment of the bank liquidity is very interesting. The bank liquidity in this case implies the ability of the bank to meet its liabilities by short-term assets.

While looking into this part of the banking activities Shenshunoff Bank recommends the following indicators:

a) **Short-term assets – Large liabilities**

Total assets

where short-term assets are cash in hand and balance on bank deposit accounts, of which: balance accruing interest + sold out federal funds and purchased securities for reselling + assets on commercial agets + debt liability with fixed rate for the terms (3 month and below + more than 3 months to 12 months) + debt liabilities with floating rate (frequency: quarterly or more frequently + annually or more frequently, but less frequently than quarterly).

Large liabilities determine the amount of term deposit certificates from USD 100 000 and more + deposits on accounts from USD 100 000 and more + deposits of foreign divisions of the bank + purchased federal funds and sold securities with repurchase + debt liabilities to the treasury with payment on request + other borrowed current assets,

b) **Large deposits with increased term**

Total assets

where large deposits with increased term are term deposit certificates from USD 100 000 and more + term deposits on accounts from USD 100 000 and more.

Depending on the group of indicators and liquidity indicators among others, the supervisory authorities in the USA assess the rating of the bank under analysis to identify the extent of supervision to be maintained towards the bank.

In the late 1990s, the Basel Committee having evaluated the extent of increasing risks issued a series of directives for risk management including the principles of assessment of liquidity management in the banking organisations.

In compliance with one representing a reliable system for internal control over the liquidity risk management needs to be established. . However, not always do credit institutions consider such a principle in their activities. "Berings" and "Credit Lionnais" are exemplary banks where adequate attention was not paid to the efficient functioning of an internal system control.

The example of many banks in the countries with transitional economies is worth mentioning because the management in these banks are not paying relevant attention to the quality of the internal control system. Whether or not a consistent document on the rules of liquidity management exists in the credit institutions could be characterised the status of the internal control system. As the practice proves, such a document does not exist in many banks, which accounts for the deterioration of the liquidity management and characterises the internal control as of low quality on the whole.

In compliance with the principles of the Basel Committee, each bank must have an agreed strategy for the liquidity management on an everyday basis and that strategy should be disseminated among all divisions the credit providing institution. To improve the quality of liquidity loss risk management, the supervisory authorities recommend reviewing the frequency of liquidity analysis set out in the document of liquidity management, and model assumptions applied in this analysis on a regular basis.

During the financial crises, prudential regulatory norms (particularly, liquidity norms) could be established by central banks and not in relative but absolute values to bring about an enhancement and reduce the deformation of the balance sheet in the various credit institutions, as well as due to the loss of the equity capital (own capital) that was the case, as for example, in Russia and Georgia in the period of 1998-1999, as well as in various countries of Eastern Europe.

Along with the sensible norms needed to regulate liquidity of the credit institutions, Central Banks also provide credits to the banks to support their current and long-term liquidity. Such a measure taken on the part of the central bank could be applied in various forms: oversight of short-term credits, credit on securities (REPO), and accommodating credit as part of financial recovery schemes, recapitalisation and restructuring of the credit institutions. Such credits could be accommodated either by central banks or the government directly via the central banks, as well as deposit insurance funds and other monetary institutions.

Central banks have lately been using monetary policy in bringing about the regulation liquidity of the credit institutions and doing this rather cautiously.

Therefore, central banks have quite a large arsenal– from prudent norms to accommodating various credits - to maintain liquidity of the credit institutions. However, it should be highlighted that along with the measures of the monetary authorities (Central Bank, Ministry of Finance, specialised funds) in maintaining the liquidity of the banking system, the quality of liquidity management inside the credit institutions is of utmost importance, and this is in terms of issues of improvements of internal control and the development and application of various models of liquidity management.

The existence of an efficient system of risk management, firstly for liquidity risks on the level of credit institutions and the banking system on the whole, creates preconditions to avert systemic banking crises and ensure sustainable and dynamic functioning of the banking system.

CHAPTER 5
The role of deposit insurance systems in banking sector sustainability and systemic banking crisis aversion

5.1. International experience of deposit insurance systems and their role in averting systemic banking crises

In the face of increasing economic instability resulting from globalisation, the development of an efficient system for ensuring financial security has been vigorously discussed by policy-makers. The financial stability forum in Basel (October 2001) identified the following essential elements of secure systems including efficient monetary and credit policy, effective oversight and the presence of a deposit insurance system.

Recently deposit insurance systems have been considered more as a remedy for banking instability than as a preventive measure. The presence of such systems ensure the maximum level of public trust in the banking sector whilst providing conditions in which stakeholders are able to be more confident in the prospects for long-term stability and return on investment in the banking sector. An efficient, functional system of guarantees encourages a responsible government role in the financial sector. This is especially true in transitional economies, where such systems are often important in strengthening market relations, reducing turnover in the shadow economy, which often involves unorganised investments of the population's savings into the banking sector of the economy while simultaneously allowing the government to maintain a social role.

The global economic and political crisis that broke out in the late 1920s led called to seek additional mechanisms to stabilise the market economy, as well as desire for a greater degree of social orientation in the banking system.

The first state deposit guarantee system emerged in the US in 1933 in compliance with the law on Banking Activities enacted in the same year as a response to the systemic banking crisis. Over a period of four years before the establishment of the Federal Deposit Insurance Corporation a total of 9,000 banks went bankrupt, amounting to one third of the total number of the banks in the country at that time. The total amount of money on deposit volume was equal to USD 6.500 million. As well as the insolvent and bankrupt banks that fell to the crisis, there were a number of sound financial institutions that also became victims of the run of the banks as across the sector, depositors panicked and demanded their deposits in cash.

The FDIC was set up to recover the confidence of depositors in the reliability of the banking system and would initially insure deposits worth up to USD 2,500. Between 1934-1937, the number of bank bankruptcies fell to 240, and the total deposits held in these banks amounted to only USD 110 million.

Following World War II, when the market economy was re-established on the principles of 'social partnership', an equilibrium between economic efficiency and social security was being established in the countries of Western Europe, the first insurance guarantee system in Western Europe was introduced in the "motherland" of the social market economy – Germany (1966), and then later in all Western European countries.

In 1994, the European Commonwealth adopted Directive # 94/19/EC 'Deposit Guarantee Schemes', which unified policy on particular key aspects of the guarantee systems, whilst leaving essential room for freedom of choice at the national level. The importance of the directive for ensuring the stability of the banking systems and economies of industrially developed countries can be compared to that of the fundamental documents of the Basel committee on regulation and supervision.

Deposit guarantee systems were gradually introduced across the world: nine systems emerged in the1960s and seven in the 1970s. Due to the escalation of crises in the 1980s, 19 more systems were created. In the 1990s, as banking crises spread across all continents, 31 more systems were created. It is important to note that in the 1990s deposit insurance systems began to emerge for the first time in countries with transitional economies.

It is also important to note that the nature of guarantee schemes varied from country to country depending on national banking law, state economic resources and conditions in the banking sector.

Deposit insurance systems based on the payment of compensation to depositors can be divided into two major categories: obligatory and voluntary.

An obligatory system of deposit guarantee functions in the great majority of countries including virtually all industrially developed countries (except Switzerland). In such cases, all stakeholders are determined by the law, as well as the management organisation, requirements on the financial status of system members, mechanisms determining the size of bank payments to form deposit insurance funds, and amounts and terms of payment to depositors.

When systems are obligatory in nature, it is almost always set up by the state. Such systems are generally managed by a special institution whose remit is to protect the owners of the insured deposits and support the financial sustainability of the system.

In the United States the Federal Deposit Insurance Corporation plays this role, in Great Britain – Deposit Insurance Funds, in Bulgaria – Banking Deposit Guarantee Fund. Under such systems, the resources of the system are mobilised at the expense of government resources, as well as through regular fees from the credit institutions.

In voluntary deposit insurance systems, the bank itself takes decision on whether or not to participate. However, not participating in the guarantee system, often requires the bank to provide additional insurance security (this might be a precondition for the issuance of a licence on certain types of transactions). At present such systems are in operation in a small number of countries (Sri Lanka, Taiwan, the Dominican Republic and a number of others). In such cases, the government does not interfere with the activities of the deposit insurance systems; neither does it offer financial support. The funds to pay the depositors' are generated only by fees provided by bank customers.

A key principle for the great majority of all deposit guarantee systems is to ensure payment of either a restricted or full amount of compensation to be paid to customers in the case of bank failure. Such systems are based on legally established procedures for the payment of bank deposits, and supported by specially created reserve funds aimed at the accumulation of resources for the repayment of deposits in times of crisis.

The difference between complete and partial compensation is clear: in the former case, the entire deposit is secured, in the latter – only part of it is, as an initially defined amount or proportion which usually has an upper ceiling. In practice across the world, the guarantee applies to all accounts held by a single depositor.

Complete compensation is guaranteed in 6 countries, including Turkey, Mexico and Ecuador among others. The majority of systems ensure only partial compensation and function in 62 countries – with the members states of the EU, the US and Canada among the largest.

The ceilings for partial compensation are determined by the level of economic development in a particular country. In the majority of developed countries and those in transition, the level of guaranteed compensation ranges from USD 376 (Tanzania) to USD 11,756 (Czech Republic). In the US, deposits are insured up to USD 100,000.

In the European Union, in compliance with Directive #94/19/EC, a minimum level of coverage is set for EU member states. The three variables for defining minimum coverage can be outlined as follows:

- A minimum guarantee level of 20,000 Euros per deposit owner; note this amount is subject to revision after the expiration of a certain period;
- A minimum guarantee level of 90 percent – subject to approval by the regulatory body on the national level;
- A minimum circle of deposit owners whose resources are subject to guarantee.

European countries are able to offer the population more favourable conditions for their deposit guarantee than the conditions stipulated in the EC Directive. They have the right to offer to their citizens guarantees exceeding the established amount of 20,000 Euros and/or offer a level of guarantee exceeding the limit of 90 percent (for example, complete compensation of the deposit amount).

Deposit guarantee systems in each country have their own peculiarities depending on the types of deposits to which these systems apply. For example, in 16 countries deposit guarantees apply only to individuals. In 20 countries the guarantees do not apply to funds in foreign currency. In a number of countries, deposits of non-residents or deposits in affiliated local banks operating in foreign states are also not covered by the system.

Regardless of whether the system is obligatory or not, fees are determined according to systems of either single or differentiated tariff rates. Differentiated systems entail differing rates depending on the liquidity, solvency and financial stability of banks, whereas single rate systems employ one rate for all institutions.

In the greater majority of the countries, fees are calculated based on the bank's liabilities on deposits. In a number of countries, for example in Norway, the total amount of assets of a bank weighed in terms of relevant legislation is applied for this purpose. All costs for fee payment are recorded as current expenditure and thus ineligible for tax.

Single rates applied in a number of countries differ significantly according to the adequacy of resources available. Standard rates applied by the majority of countries employing such systems vary from 0.1 to 0.5 percent of the deposit amount. Depending on the financial status of a particular bank, the state of the banking system and the presence of relevant financial resources for the guarantee system, the rates could be even higher. For example, in Macedonia the fee rate in the guarantee fund is 1.5 percent, in Turkey – 1.2 percent, in Romania – 0.6 percent and in Peru - 1.45 percent.

Insured accident accounting for the compensation usually emerges in case of bankruptcy. Under these circumstances, the deposit guarantee system takes over the assets and liabilities of the failed bank and starts compensating depositors in compliance with a predefined set of rules. After insured payments are made, the deposit guarantee fund realises the assets of the failed bank, covering its costs from the resources generated and meeting the failed bank's remaining liabilities.

Since the establishment of a deposit guarantee system in the USA, the accelerated procedure for the administrative closure of banks is exercised without the need for the initiation of legal bankruptcy proceedings. The Federal Deposit Insurance Corporation acquires complete control over the bankrupt bank, and has the right to replace its management and carry out bank restructuring either by forcing a merger or via the transfer of the assets and liabilities of the failed bank to itself.

Deposit guarantee systems are also able to take certain preventive measures to apply influence on banks whose financial status is a subject for concern.

FDIC in the US is authorised to exclude those banks carrying out illegal or risky transactions from the insurance system. Furthermore, to ensure the protection of the depositors' interests, it holds the right to render assistance to the bank at an early stage through the purchase of assets and loan extensions in order to avert the bank's bankruptcy.

International practice demonstrates that the financial support of the state is important in the maintenance of a sustainable deposit insurance system. The range of forms of state participation in deposit insurance systems, with regard to the variety of legislation in a number of countries can be illustrated using the following examples:

In Austria, when all other sources of finance for the insurance system have been exhausted, the state issues bonds secured by the Austrian Government.

In Great Britain, the deposit guarantee system is able to borrow up to 175 million pounds from the Bank of England . Amendment # 64 of the Banking Act of 1986 provides the basis for obtaining the aforementioned resources. If this is insufficient and the threat of systemic crisis is regarded as tangible, the state is able to interfere despite the lack of formal legislation to enable it to do so.

In Greece, the government provided the guarantee fund with its start-up capital. The Fund has the right to ask banks to pay additional fees (up to triple the size of the ordinary annual fee).

In Denmark, the Ministry of Economic Activities is able to act as a guarantor to extend necessary additional resources to the deposit guarantee system.

In Ireland, Spain, Iceland, the Netherlands and Finland borrowings from the Central Bank are permitted only in exceptional cases.

When the Deposit Insurance Corporation was established in Japan in 1971, the government contributed 5.15 billion Yen to its authorised capital with the Bank of Japan contributing 150 million Yen.

According to various sources, in the US, during the Savings and Loan Association crisis of the 1980s, USD 200-500 billion was allocated to the deposit guarantee system from the budget. The Law of 1991, on

Refinancing, Structural Modification and Improvement of the Federal Corporation of Reorganisation envisaged additional financing for this corporation from the budget to the amount of USD 25 billion.

In Hungary and Poland, the accumulation of resources is possible through the provision of credit from the Central Bank.

Although no formal support to the deposit guarantee system is provided by the government in Italy, Lichtenstein and Luxemburg, in reality such assistance is usually rendered when necessary.

The analysis of the recent trends in the development of deposit insurance systems is essential in order to fully understand the role of this financial instrument in the modern world.

Firstly, in recent years the world has witnessed an increase in the number of deposit guarantee systems on all continents. In Europe, their number increased from 23 in 1995 to 32 in 1999 largely due to the establishment of systems in transition countries.

In Europe, Africa and America, the number of countries that take into consideration risk while determining the amount of obligatory fees paid by financial institutions is increasing. Today this approach is used by almost 30 percent of countries with functioning deposit guarantee systems.

An important trend in the way deposit guarantee systems are implemented is also noticeable: more and more deposit guarantee systems have become obligatory. Today eight out of ten countries have obligatory systems while in the mid-1990s this ratio was 50/50. Adoption of the EU Directive #94/19/EC has driven this trend in Europe whilst promoting the practice worldwide. Similar processes are also underway in the Middle East and Latin America.

Interestingly the systems with accumulation deposit funds are given preference though. Although the countries with the systems of obligatory fees according to actual fact did not transfer to the system with accumulation fund, newly formed systems have necessary reserves.

The insurance systems whose financial activities are based on the accumulation fund exist in all countries of Africa and Asia. Eighty percent of the total number of functioning deposit guarantee systems today comprises such funds. It is generally acknowledged that the systems with accumulation funds are more sustainable and adequate to the modern risk level.

The tendency towards increased state participation in guarantee systems is especially important. Though most of the systems today are still financed by private contributions, the number of systems able to obtain additional financial support from the state under emergency economic conditions is increasing. More than 75 percent of the current operational systems are able to obtain assistance from government, if deemed necessary.

The EC Directive is also responsible for growing standardisation in the amount of compensation available. This applies particularly to EU member states and those countries currently seeking to become part of the bloc.

Almost all countries today try to link compensation to the deposit owner and not to a particular deposit, which is reflected in a tendency towards lowered levels of compensation.

The number of the systems guaranteeing payment of compensation only to private persons and non-profit organisations is also increasing. These restrictions are currently in use by around one quarter of all countries with such systems, up from only 13 percent in 1995 .

The number of systems excluding inter-bank deposits from compensation schemes has grown substantially (from 45 percent to 66 percent). These changes have been implemented both in Europe (in compliance with the EU Directive) in addition to other countries on other continents.

The tendency towards excluding currency deposits from the guarantee system is also noticeable, this trend could probably be attributed to the increase in currency risks. In 1999, 40 percent of countries excluded all or some deposits in foreign currency from the guarantee system.

Therefore, taking into consideration world trends, the establishment of efficient deposit insurance systems is becoming increasingly crucial for countries in transition. Such institutions are an essential part of any set of instruments for crisis aversion. However it should be noted that the efficiency of any deposit insurance system will significantly depend on many national factors.

World practice demonstrates that unless a deposit insurance system is endowed with supervisory functions over credit institutions, and the ability to restructure and liquidate troubled banks, the efficiency of such systems will be questionable.

Furthermore, the efficiency of a deposit insurance system depends considerably on the quality of two other major aspects a country's financial security: weighted monetary and credit policy and banking supervision arranged in compliance with internationally recognised standards.

5.2. Principles and approaches of establishment of a deposit insurance system in Georgia

In recent years deposit insurance systems have continued to be established in many transitional countries. The formation of such institutes is attributed to the generalisation of the regrettable lessons of systemic banking crises; such systems are established with the aim of protecting fragile emerging economies.

This process is also vital for Georgia. This chapter recommends that a system be established based on the following principles.

The deposit insurance system must be obligatory.

To ensure maximum financial sustainability of this system, active support from the government, and the opening of a special credit line from the National Bank of Georgia to ensure liquidity in the system's finances are crucial.

It is also important that uniform mandatory rate levels for the bulk of commercial banks be established, with differentiated rates available for more risky banks.

The combination of obligatory and voluntary deposit insurance has proved its efficiency in many countries, such as Germany, Finland and Austria.

To create a deposit insurance system, particular social and economic conditions are definitely necessary. Due to the vulnerability of Georgia's economy, an objective necessity can be seen; making the creation of such a system inevitable.

One of the key tasks of the Deposit Insurance Fund shall be (along with compensation for depositors in the case of bank failure), ensuring consistent functioning of banks through the taking of measures to recover their solvency. This organisation therefore has to be empowered by relevant authorities supported by the rule of law.

The Deposit Insurance Fund shall accept the authority of bank creditor in the disbursement of key assets as practiced in many countries. Direct participation in the reimbursement of receivables from insolvent banks is the basis for the creation of a subdivision coordinating the restructuring and liquidation of problem credit institutions. It is necessary that depositors of insolvent banks are paid up to a predetermined level or the deposits be transferred to problem-free banks along with the part of the liquidated bank's assets.

Quarterly payments from banks into a guarantee fund will increase the conventional value of attracted deposits. Theoretically banks would be able to compensate for the rise in costs by a corresponding increase in their revenues from their assets, but this is possible only at the expense of and increased risk in active transactions. On the other hand, the growth in cost of the payments could be prevented by lowering the deposit rates on the deposits of customers; however, this could result in a deposit outflow from the banks participating in the deposit guarantee system.

Therefore, it is considered essential to identify a number of measures that aim to compensate banks – members of the Fund – for their additional costs accrued through payment of the fees to the guarantee fund. A reduction in the norm for obligatory reserves, or either a reduction of or exemption from a number of mandatory taxes in the local budget, etc. would support these measures. This will help to avoid a drop in profitability linked to outgoings for fee payments, and reduced confidence predetermined by increase in risk of the credit and investment policy for participants. Concurrently, this will release the banks from the necessity to reduce the rate for mobilisation of funds that will avert outflow of depositors.

If a deposit insurance system is established in Georgia, all recent trends in the development of the deposit insurance systems across the world must be taken into consideration, as well as the pre-existing social and economic situation in the country.

CHAPTER 6
Recent global economic crises

6.1. How to overcome banking problems in Georgia

In contemporary Georgia the banking sector has emerged as one of the most successful and dynamically developing segments of the economy. Since 1995, with the assistance of various international financial institutes (International Monetary Fund, World Bank, European Bank of Reconstruction and Development and others), the banking system has been growing and developing according to international standards and, during the period 2005-2007, the annual growth of banking assets reached 60-65% on average being the highest indicator for the last period.

Official international reserves of the National Bank of Georgia for 7 months in 2008 increased by 7.6% and equalled USD 1,465 million.

For the first time since October 2007, the official inflation indicator fell below the two-digit figure and, by the end of July 2008, stood at 9.8% (Pic. 1). Nevertheless, note the average inflation indicator for the last years tended to grow (2003 – 4.8%, 2004 – 5.7%, 2005 – 8.3%, 2006 – 9.2%, 2007 – 8.2%, 7 months of 2008 -11.2%). In July 2006 annual indicator of inflation reached 14.5%. After 2005 it was obvious that inflation acquired a chronic nature in Georgia.

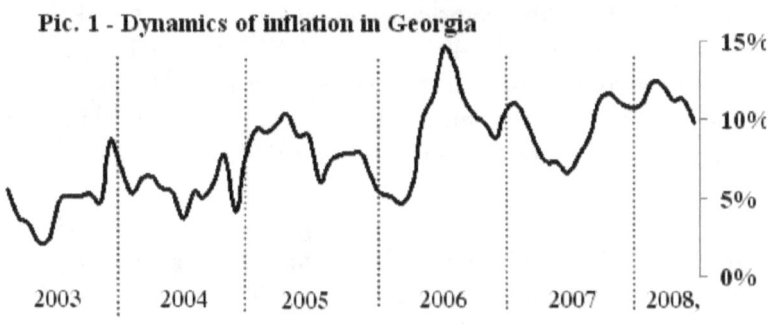

Pic. 1 - Dynamics of inflation in Georgia

Starting from 2003 the dollarisation coefficient of deposits tended to gradually decrease. Despite this trend its level still remains high. At the end of July 2008, it equalled 60.5%. Concurrently it was especially high in terms of ordinary people's savings, which accounted for 73.3% of all deposits. Another significant trend that was noticed in the first half of 2008 refers to the structure of currency deposits. By the end of 2002 97% of currency deposits were in US Dollars, while the share of deposits in Euros was only 3%. Later the Euro became more popular amongst depositors and, by the end of July 2008, the volume of Euro deposits among currency deposits comprised 30%.

The average growth rate of assets in the banking sector during 2000-2004 was within 15-23%. After 2004 the growth rate significantly increased and, in 2005, it was 39%, in 2006 it stood at 67%, in 2007 the rate was 71% and, in the first seven months of 2008 the growth rate was 41%. By the end of July 2007 the banking assets had increased 5.2 times compared to figures available for the end of 2004. Due to a relatively high growth rate compared to GDP, the bank assets and GDP ratio lately has grown (2003: 15.6%, 2004: 17.3%, 2005: 21.9%, 2006: 30.7%, 2007: 42.4%). It is estimated that if this growth rate is maintained, the growth of the banking sector of Georgia will approach the level of Central and Eastern European countries.

Other indicators are also going up: in the same comparison period net loans increased six-fold, gross deposits increased 3.6 times, gross deposits of ordinary savers 3.7 times (o/w term deposits 3.6 times),

173

borrowings 8.5 times, and capital increased 5 times compared to the level at the end of 2004. Note the significant growth in gross deposits of ordinary people, from GEL 493 million to GEL 1,831 million, perhaps indicating a positive trend in the recovery of trust by the population in the banking system. If at the end 2000 deposits of physical persons comprised 39% of gross deposits, as of July 2007 it equalled 44%.

Other financial indicators of the banking system grew in a relative manner. In 2004 gross income of the commercial banks was GEL 276 million, and net profit GEL 27 million, in 2007 it equalled GEL 949 and 109 million, respectively. In 2007, banks paid GEL 302 million (of which GEL 126 million on term deposits) as interest. Significant changes also occurred in the structure of income and expenditure of banks. In 2007 compared to 2004, the share of interest income in gross income grew from 56% to 73%. Also, in 2004 the interest expense in gross expenses was 18%; in 2007 it comprised 32%. Correspondingly non-interest expense share decreased from 67% to 40% (including the share for office maintenance – from 23% to 19%).

Although the share of key players in the banking market of Georgia still remains high, it shows a downward tendency. In early 2007 the relative share of the two largest banks was 58.8%, by the end of July it decreased to 57.2%, and the share of the top five banks (Bank of Georgia, TBC Bank, Republic Bank, ProCredit Bank and VTB Bank) decreased from 85.5% to 82.9%.

Starting from 2007, the competition in the banking market grew. Banks were rigorously opening new branches and service centres. In just the last year and a half their number increased by 52% and by the end of July 2008 it comprised 640 (of which 129 were branches and 511 – service centres). Along with opening branches and service centres, new products and services were being offered. A large portion of banks extended working hours (from 9am till 10pm) and service centres emerged which operated around the clock. Compared to previous years the quality of credit accessibility improved significantly. Small consumer and installment loans were obtainable without additional guarantees. Retail outlets, car traders and construction businesses were actively involved in the process of encouraging consumers to borrow money, and the number of mortgage loan agreements also blossomed. Additionally the banks began to either buy out existing insurance companies, or else set up their own. The number and diversity of electronic services also extended. In the first seven months of 2008 the number of cash dispensers increased by 43%, totalling 1,189. During the same period the number of post-terminals increased by 40% to 7,253. The number of debit cards increased by 43% and reached 2.7 million issues, and the number of credit cards increased by 165% to over 427 thousand issues.

Along with increase of economic activity and competition between banks in recent years, interest rates on deposits and credits in Georgia naturally went down. However, this trend slowed and, by 2005, the trend reversed both on deposits and bank loans (Pic. 2). It was also natural that the banks started to increase interest rates, first on deposits (starting from late-2004), and an increase in the value of resources and high inflation caused credits to go up in price from late 2005. This process was especially tangible from July 2007. The market interest rate on loans over 12 months increased by 4.6 units and, by July 2008, reached 22.2% (which is 26% growth).

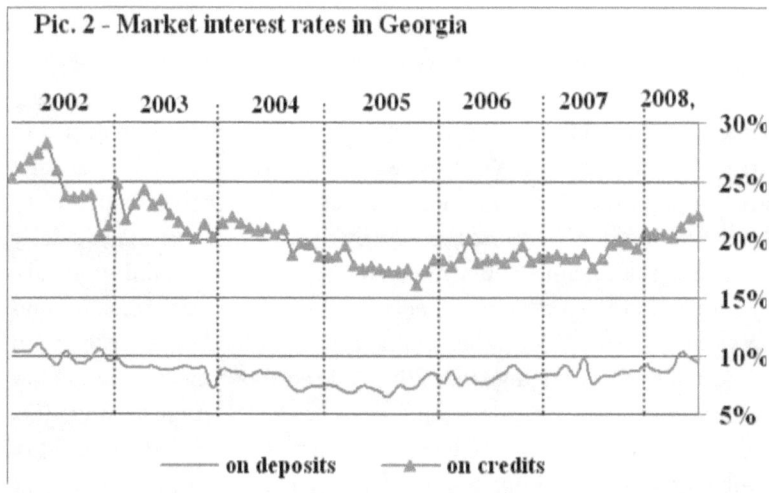

Pic. 2 - Market interest rates in Georgia

It was obvious that although interest rates had been increased and huge resources had been invested to carry out various marketing measures (promotional campaigns, introducing grace periods and lotteries, etc.), banks found it more and more difficult to attract resources on both the domestic and foreign markets, and to satisfy increased demand on credits. The share of loans in the consolidated assets of the banking system was going up. For example, average net loans and average net assets ratio in 1999-2004 did not exceed 52%, the same indicator by the end of July 2008 had reached 61%. This of course, led to a corresponding and quite significant decrease of the share of liquid resources in the bank assets and an increase in risks, both, in the entire banking system and in individual banks.

In 2006-2007 the average growth rate indicator of the bank credit portfolios was 4.2% per month, whereas between February and July 2008 it comprised 3.3%; of which 2.6% occurred between May and July. During the same time period the low level of attraction of resources on the local market is more obvious. The growth rate of gross deposits in 2006-2007 comprised 3.6%, including 1.5% between February and July 2008, of which 1.1% occurred between May and July and, in case of deposits, 3.3%, 2.5% and 1.7% in the relevant periods. Furthermore, during 2008 there were months when these indicators tended to decline, for example, gross deposits in the month of February decreased by 2.5% and ordinary savings deposits by 0.5%. In other words, activity in the banking sector during the last year was certainly decelerating.

As a result the banks demonstrated negative tendencies with regard to attraction of resources. We have witnessed the outcome that usually accompanies the above mentioned process, if the banks' supervisory bodies do not intervene and regulate by relevant leverages. Particularly of note is that, before 2004, monetary resources (cash and monetary resources on the correspondent accounts) ratio to assets, net loans and total liabilities in 1999-2004 retained stability (and even went up, in some cases) but , starting from 2005, all the above-mentioned quality indicators tend to deteriorate and, even before the August events (i.e. the war between Georgia & Russia), there were quite evident liquidity problems in the banking system (Pic. 3). The indicator of monetary resource and net loans ratio between the end of 2004 and the end of July 2008 declined from 60% to 33%, including declines in liabilities (from 40% to 25%) and from 31% to 20% in assets.

Pic. 3 - Dynamics of banking system liquidity indicators in Georgia

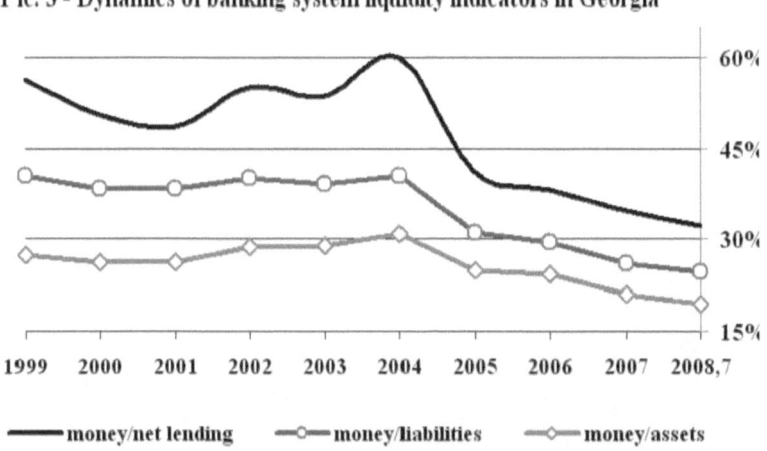

money/net lending　　money/liabilities　　money/assets

Concurrently, the deposit average term indicator, which is one of the indicators determining the population's degree of confidence towards banks, starts to decline. During the period spanning 1996-1999 the average term indicator of term deposits was 6.9 months, and this increased significantly from early 2002 and equalled to 9 months (Pic.4). After certain 'failures' 2003 witnessed an improvement that lasted until early 2004 and comprised 12.3 months. This is the only period when the average term of term deposits exceeded the average term of loans. However, after that period the average term for term deposits demonstrates a permanent downward trend (with small exceptions) and it decreased back down to 9 months by the end of July 2008.

However, the indicator of loan terms tended to grow and, in the period from early 2000 to early 2008 increased from 8.6 months to 14.7 months although, during 2008 it remained at a steady level. It is apparent that discrepancy between assets and liabilities (in the part of deposits) in regard with the term in the banking system deteriorates GAP of the banking system and particular banks. Certainly the average term on loans and deposits does not necessarily equal but the fact that they are fluctuating not in parallel but in the opposite directions is problematic.

Pic. 4 - Avarage term of credits and deposits in Georgia (month)

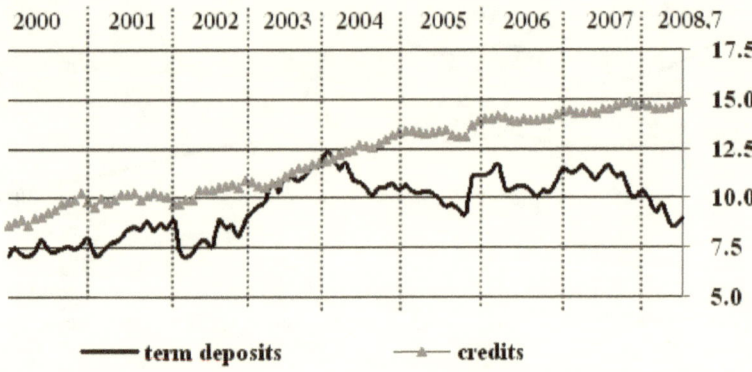

Finally, if we compare two trends in regard to the deposits attracted by banks – average term decrease on term deposits and deposit interest rate growth, it becomes obvious that it demonstrates, on the one hand, problems with resource attraction and liquidity, and with making resources more expensive and deterioration of financial indicators, on the other. As a result despite the fact that recently the banks were generating more income, the indicator of profitability was declining. In 2002-2007 ROA (Return on Assets, i.e. profit on assets) on average was 3.1, in 7 months of 2007 it dropped to 1.7. ROE (Return on Equity, i.e. profit on capital) fell from 13.5 to 8.3 in the corresponding period. One more negative trend that emerged prior to the August events is connected with the recent deterioration in the quality of the bank loan portfolio. During the last few years the ratio between banking system loan potential loss reserves and the credit investment volume was declining and, by July 2007, had dropped to 3.3%. The share of the outstanding loans in the gross portfolio by then was 0.7. In the subsequent 12 months the credit portfolio quality significantly deteriorated and the ratio of the above mentioned reserves and the credit portfolio increased by 4.3% and the share of the outstanding loans – by 1.7%.

One thing is clear, even *before* the well publicised events of August 2008 the banking system of Georgia was already facing substantial problems which were both sizeable and obvious. True, the banking system of Georgia endured the additional strains placed upon it during the wartime but the above mentioned events deepened the problems even more. The August crisis had a significant impact on the banking system of Georgia and on the economy in general. The assets of the banking system between August and October 2008 declined by GEL 1,026 million (13%), and the losses of the banking system as of January 1st, 2009 comprised GEL 215 million. The conflict actually exposed all of the inner banking contradictions and disproportions which existed prior to that period and, between September to November, when the world economic and financial crises further developed, these disproportions deepened further, dramatically affecting the short and middle-term development of Georgian banking sector.

There are certain opinions on what the priority should be in the current situation. It is obvious that the Banks' Supervisory Service has to operate in a more flexible and adequate manner. Whilst respecting the confidential aspects of the banking system this Service along with the National Bank of Georgia has to work more transparently in every direction. Also everybody should try that the participation of the international financial institutes in the Georgian banks becomes stronger, consequently it is desirable to identify strategic investor in the leading banks

It is essential that the best practices of corporate governance be implemented in the Georgian banks, and it is particularly important that the functions of the Supervisory Board and management be distinguished, and an independent director introduced in the banks. The further process of consolidation and merger in the banking system shall be encouraged.

Reflecting on these issues, developing complex approaches and implementing them quickly and prudentially shall trigger the improvement of the system and encourage its further development.

6.2. Global economic crises: reasons for the problems and the ways of overcoming them

Imbalances in the economy which have accumulated in recent years, shortcomings in the institutional sphere (primarily in regulation and supervision), growth of competition and interdependence of countries as a result of the development of globalisation made the large-scale global economic crisis inevitable. Famous economists, particularly, J. Stiglitz, N. Roubini, P. Krugman, warned about the advancement of such a crisis. Roubini, who is Professor of economy at the Stern School of Business, clearly stated the following: "It's pretty clear by now that this is the worst financial crisis, economic crisis and recession since the Great Depression. A number of us were worrying about it a while ago. At this point it's becoming conventional wisdom."

In 2008, the growth rate of the most important economic indicator, GDP, in the majority of the developed countries fell significantly; furthermore, starting from the third and fourth quarters of 2008, these countries entered recession. Growth rate of GDP in 2008 comprised 1.1% in the USA, -0.6% in Japan, 0.7% in the UK, 0.5% in Canada, 0.9% - in the eurozone, comprised of 1.3% in Germany, 0.7% in France, and -1% in Italy.

International financial organisations including the IMF and the World Bank forecast a rather dramatic drop of GDP in the developed countries and in the majority of the developing countries in 2009. According to the IMF forecast the world GDP in 2009 will decrease by 1.3% overall, and by 3.8% in the developed countries. The recession in the USA will be – 2.8%, Japan – 6.2%, Great Britain – 4.1%, Canada – 2.5%, Germany – 5.6%, France – 3%, Italy – 4.4%. In certain developed countries the rate of GDP drop is anticipated to reach very high level, for example, in Ireland it will equal 8%, in Iceland 10.6% and, in Singapore, 10%.

Moreover, rather a dramatic decrease of GDP in the first quarter of 2009 gives grounds to even more pessimistic forecasts. In Q1 2009 GDP in the USA dropped by 2.6%, in Great Britain by 4.1%, in France by 3.2%, in Germany by 6.9%, and by 5.9% in Italy. Concurrently, the figures demonstrating industrial recession are even more shocking reaching 11.7% in the USA, 32.9% in Japan, 19.8% in Germany and 18.4% in France, during the first quarter of 2009.

The crisis was noticeable in the decrease of such an important constituent of GDP as consumer spending. In 2008, it increased in the developed countries only by 0.6%, and according to the IMF forecast, it will drop by 1.4% in 2009. Another component of GDP, the formation of the fixed capital, decreased by 1.8% in the developed countries in 2008, and according to the IMF forecast in 2009, it will decrease by 12.5%.

It is no surprise that such a significant reduction of GDP and, especially, of industrial production led to a growth in unemployment. According to the IMF forecast unemployment in the developed countries will increase to 8.1% in 2009 (in 2008 it was at the level of 5.8%). In 2009, in the USA the level of unemployment equalled 8.9%, in Japan it reached 4.6%, in Great Britain 7.4%, in Germany 9%, in France 9.6% and, in Italy, 8.9%. In some of the developed countries this indicator reached even higher levels, notably 17.7% in Spain, 11.5% in Slovakia, 12% in Ireland and 9.7% in Iceland. According to Roubini's estimates, in the USA "the rate of unemployment rate this year is going to be above 10%, and is likely to be close to 11% next year. Thus, next year is still going to feel like a recession, even if we're technically out of the recession".

The economic crisis has also affected world trade. According to IMF forecasts, in 2009, for the first time in the post-war period, world trade will substantially slow down (by 11%). In the developed countries exports are expected to drop by 13.5% and imports by 12.1%.

According to the IMF predictions the level of savings and investments will noticeably reduce. In 2007, the level of savings in the developed countries (as a percentage of GDP) was 20.5%, in 2008 it dropped to 19.4% and in 2009 it will go as low as 17.4%. Note that, in the key economy (the US), this indicator is expected to equal just 11.9% in 2009. The level of savings in the Euro zone is anticipated to be 18.8%, including 19.5% in Germany, 20.4% in France, and 15.7% in Italy. Investment in various countries reduced from 21.3% in 2007 to 20.8%

in 2008 and, still further, to 18.3% in 2009. However, in the USA this indicator in 2009 will comprise 14.7%, in the Euro area – 19.7%, of which in Germany – 17.2%, in France – 19.9%, in Italy – 18.8%.

However the crisis in the financial sphere, i.e. in the foreign exchange markets, stock exchanges, and in the banking and insurance sectors of economy, was the most acute.

As a result of the crisis a number of the largest financial institutes in the USA collapsed, particularly the investment bank Lehman Brothers. Mortgage companies Fannie Mae, Freddie Mac and the largest American insurance company AIG turned out to be on the verge of collapse.

Many of the European insurance companies and banks incurred initial and substantial losses from investments in the sub-prime mortgage market. Net losses of the largest Netherlands financial and insurance company ING Groep N.V. comprised Euros 729 million in 2008, and the net profit of Commerzbank equalled only Euros 3 million. Net losses of Swiss bank UBS AG in 2008 was Euros 13.09 billion, and of the Bank Credit Suisse – Euros 5.45 billion. On the whole current losses of the world banking sector as a result of the crisis are assessed at USD 4 trillion.

The crisis was demonstrated through an exceptional drop in the value of financial assets reaching USD 50 trillion in 2008, according to the assessment of the Asian Bank of Development.

The crisis is also hallmarked by the significant depreciation of many currencies, including those of the developed countries. Virtually all countries suffered from the increase in the deficit of their state budget and public debt.

The crisis became global, permeating all sectors of the economy and virtually all countries causing social and political upheaval which led to a change in government, in some countries.

If we analyse the origins of this crisis, we can distinguish the following groups of factors: macro-economic, microeconomic including ideology and practice of running the business, and institutional.

Whilst analysing the macro-economic factors, the key moment is the ideology of the macro-economic policy that has been dominant for the last 20-30 years. This policy rested on an economic theory that envisaged unlimited efficiency, priority of short term goals and factors in the economy, transfer of the market approach to the analysis of all economic structures and problems. As a result, the macroeconomic policy of the monetary power not only did not limit the inflation of "bubbles" on the financial and credit markets, but at a certain extent even stimulated it by extending ever growing credit resources to the financial institutes without considering actual risks and consequences of such an automatic refinancing. The development of the credit and financial spheres, including the expansion of the volumes of the financial and credit instruments, significantly outstripped the development of the real sector of the economy. The development of the money and financial markets was more and more oriented on making short-term speculative gain and accumulating risks.

If we analyse the statistics of the financial markets, we will see that in 2004, the total volume of debt securities in issue in the world economy comprised USD 13270 billion, and in 2005 it increased to USD 13951 billion. In 2006 this indicator comprised USD 17545 billion, in 2007 – USD 21578 billion, in 2008 (the first half of the year) – USD 23886 billion. Therefore, the volume of debt securities almost doubled in 5 years.

The increase of the volume of issued derivatives was even faster. In just two years (from June 2006 to June 2008) the value of the issued derived financial instruments increased from USD 370 trillion to USD 684 trillion, i.e. almost twice.

Bubble blowing was also prevalent in the credit sphere. Macroeconomic policy in a number of the leading developed countries in recent years included large scale credit expansion, on the mistaken assumption that large scale encouragement of consumer spending, especially via mortgages, would ensure additional and stable economic growth.

Particularly during the period when interest rates were very low banks and other financial institutes, making the most of what could be termed as *automatic refinancing*, directed these resources towards offering easily available credit to promote spending, whilst ignoring the rather high risks.

For example, mortgage arrears in the USA went up from USD 9,353 billion in 2003 to USD 14,565 billion in 2007, i.e. more than 1.5 times. Concurrently, according to the Mortgage Bankers Association the share of the credits on which the payment were outstanding at least once, reached 7.88% of the total mortgage credits being a historical maximum. Furthermore, more than 8.3 million Americans who took mortgage credits have debts that exceed the actual value of their dwellings.

Based on the potential "toxic" assets various financial instruments used to be issued in which many financial institutes eagerly invested their resources since these investments allowed to earn rapid profit, distribute high bonuses to the managers and ensure the same high dividends for the shareholders. Renowned Hungarian-American financier George Soros efficiently summarised such a macroeconomic policy: "Let's face it, for twenty-five years we have been consuming more than we have been producing. This living beyond our means accumulated mainly in the housing sector and the financial sector, and now those liabilities are being nationalised".

The trends are the same in other segments of crediting. For example, the volume of syndicated crediting in the world in four years (2004 -2007) increased from USD 1,347 billion to USD 2,667 billion, i.e. twice.

Among negative macroeconomic trends leading to the crisis could be named sweeping capitalisation of the exchange markets, avalanche-type growth of the exchange transactions and the large scale issuance of new financial instruments.

As a consequence, destructive processes abounded in the world economy. This situation was very eloquently characterised by a famous specialist in crises caused by financial globalisation, professor at Geneva University

E. Fontela: "The characteristics of the modern economy depend on the relative power of two mutually complementary subsystems – financial and "real". A substantial upheaval characteristic for the modern post-industrial era is in the change of their correlation: the leadership from the "captains of the industry" moves to the financiers, the profit is not necessarily the result of the development and production improvement, it could easily be the outcome of the financial transactions for which one needs the "speculative spirit" rather than the "entrepreneurial spirit"... A logical question emerges regarding the practicality of such changes from the point of view of real and not the "paper" world well-being".

Formation of an ultraliberal economic model wherein the domination of the financial sphere and short-term economic goals occurred simultaneously with the enhancement of globalisation led to encompassing more and more new countries and regions.

Globalisation and economic liberalisation envisaged unlimited capital movement among others. Theoretically liberalisation of the financial sector and international financial inflows has to ensure optimisation of allocation of limited resources. However, in practice along with some benefits, liberalisation and globalisation brought to a large dependence of the national economies on the rapid flows of "hot money". It was especially obvious in the developing countries and countries in transition. One famous specialist in the problems of globalisation, Nobel Memorial Prize Winner in Economic Sciences Joseph E. Stiglitz, analysing the crises in the Asian countries in the late 1990s characterised this process as follows: "Though the countries of the region did not have any needs in additional capital due to high savings, the liberalisation of capital accounts was imposed on them in the late 1980s - early 1990s. I am sure that this liberalisation of the capital account was the only most important factor that led to the crisis. Very often the liberalisation of the capital account is a risk without the relevant remuneration".

Furthermore, in the conditions of globalisation new economic centres tended to develop very rapidly (e.g. India and China, etc.) leading to the growth of imbalances in world trade. Increase in the deficit of balance of trade and payment in the number of countries along with the growth of their public debt became one more negative trend triggering the global crisis.

It is also worth mentioning that a rapid increase in the price of the raw materials in 2006-2008, which led to the enhancement of imbalances in world trade and the global economy, caused intensification of inflation, growth of costs of production and, eventually, played an important role in the emergence of the global crisis.

Along with a set of macroeconomic reasons there are also institutional factors which contribute to the global crisis.

The determining factor for that is a long and large scale process of deregulation that affected all the sectors of the economy but, most fundamentally, in the financial sector. Deregulation was going on as a backdrop to the rapid development of advanced technologies and emergence of new types of financial products and a sharp growth in the volume of financial transactions, including exchange, stock markets trades and futures. As a result entire segments of the economy were practically beyond regulation; regulating norms were seriously legging behind the changes on the market. The eminent American economist P. Krugman figuratively and unequivocally characterised a long process of deregulation: "All of this high finance has turned out to be just destructive, and that's partly a matter of regulation. Because as the financial sector got increasingly bloated its political clout also grew. So, in fact, deregulation bred bloated finance, which bred more deregulation, which bred this monster that ate the world economy".

The emergence of global financial pyramids highlights the poor standards of quality and efficiency of regulation. Large scale capital laundering via off-shore financial centres has also become an acute problem. In their attempts to combat this, the governments of many developed countries were forced to take special measures. Hence, in the conditions of globalisation inadequacy of regulation on the international level became especially evident.

Another institutional factor of the crisis was the fact that a number of institutes whose duties were regulation were not up to the mark. In the conditions of deregulation, rapid growth of markets and technologies, accumulation of systemic risks the problem of informational asymmetry was becoming more and more acute (according to the opinion of many famous economists, particularly Stiglitz and also J. Akerlof, this was one of the most important reasons for economic crises). Investors and creditors were objectively in need of adequate and realistic information about the level of risk, financial status of issuers and counteragents; however, existing institutes whose duties were to resolve this problem, particularly, rating agencies, informational-analytical centres from specific fields, consulting and audit companies, credit bureaus, to a large extent did not execute their functions. Leading rating agencies were subjected to tough criticism from society and government bodies of the developed countries; and there were even some attempts to place the blame for the crisis on them. However, these institutes became hostages of the dominant model of the development of financial markets, which assumed that there were no risks in investing in these or other assets, certain automation of rating evaluations, the market participants blindly followed the assessments provided by leading rating agencies.

Along with macroeconomic and institutional factors of the crisis, we cannot avoid mentioning the factors at the level of macro-economy. Firstly, this is the strife of the companies and banks towards short-lived profit without adequate consideration of possible risks. Many companies and banks started to vigorously develop sub-divisions dealing with financial transactions, and very often traditional aspects of business were deprived of adequate attention. As a result financial institutes and companies started to precariously depend on the price fluctuations on the world markets and on the inflows of speculative capital. The system governing risk management was not adequate either, as that was too much oriented on external evaluations.

Furthermore, the policy of allocating resources (high risky credits, investments in the derivative and mortgage financial instruments) not commensurate to the risks, also capitalisation not relevant to actual risks was observed in the banking sector. All these problems were acutely revealed in the conditions of crisis when even the largest global banks found themselves in a rather difficult financial situation. The results of stress-testing recently conducted by the monetary authorities of the U.S. revealed inadequacy of capital in a number of the largest American banks.

Hence, multiple of factors of macro-economic, institutional and microeconomic nature led to the most dramatic crisis in the last 70 years.

Despite the difficult situation we cannot but mention that monetary authorities of virtually all the developed countries (as well as of many developing countries) did their best to mitigate the consequences of the crisis by providing tremendous support to the banking sector in the forms of recapitalisation, refinancing, providing liquidity, measures for encouraging consumer demand and support to the real sector of the economy.

Especially large scale financial assistance to the economy was rendered in the USA. In the autumn of 2008, the U.S. Congress approved a plan proposed by the Ministry of Finance for the stabilisation of the U.S. financial system which envisaged the allocation of USD 700 billion to buy out problem debts from the banks. Later, U.S. President Barak Obama signed a stimulation package of the economy for an additional USD 787 billion that also included tax reduction and an increase in expenditure on government projects. Large scale financial assistance was also rendered to the real sector of the economy, particularly to automobile manufacturers.

To resist the crisis, the central banks of the developed countries successively reduced the rates for refinancing, as a result it reached the historical minimum in virtually all countries; transactions to buy out assets from commercial banks would also be carried out.

In April 2009, at the G20 meeting in London, a programme on how to overcome the crisis was approved. The programme included such directions as forecasting and averting crises in the future, financial assistance to the global economy, including use of the IMF, tackling the "tax oasis" problem, regulation of bonus payments to company and bank executives, measures to support national economies and tightening of controls over financial markets.

Each of these directions call for more detailed analysis including the forecast of tentative outcomes.

The discussions among the economists and politicians about the importance of forecasting the crises have been going on for a long time. Certain steps had been made, institutes had been set up, for example, Forum of Financial Stability. At the meeting of the G20 countries it was decided to create an efficient system of forecasting economic crises and formation of a new Council of Financial Stability that would incorporate all of the G20 countries, all the members of the Forum of Financial Stability and the European Commission. The goal of this institute, as it was formulated by Prime Minister of the United Kingdom Gordon Brown is "to change the way our regulating system works so that financial powers could identify and take measures to avert the risks. The Council shall enhance regulation and observance over all the important from the system point of view financial institutes, instruments and markets".

Recently in the political and economic circles the proposals have been made for the creation of sustainable economies which would be able to develop without the sort of cyclic fluctuations which have been discussed.

Approved decisions and announcements indicate that dismantlement of the macro-economic model dominating in the recent decade, which was based on the usefulness of deregulation, trust in self-regulation and in the high efficiency of pure market mechanisms, is proceeding rather rapidly. However, while the new macro-economic policy is in the process of formation, it is not yet clear how much the role of the state will be enhanced, how the methods of macro-economic forecasting will be applied in practice. Announced goals call for certain transformations within the regulatory and other institutes, and for the formation of relevant instruments and procedures. It should be mentioned that the idea of stronger and more efficient regulation is met with resistance by some of the participants of the market.

The very idea of economic development without any crisis is considered rather naive and practically unachievable due to the natural imbalances at any market (for example, between demand and supply). To a certain extent such imbalances are characteristic of the market economy, their appearance makes the participants of the market review their strategy and tactics of doing business, leads to the inter-sector and inter-regional spill-over of the capital and growth of production effectiveness. True, these market mechanisms, this "invisible hand" by A. Smith, work and at a certain extent are the basis for the market economy.

However, in the post-industrial society the role of the state (in the national economy) and international institutes (in the global economy) is to manage such market processes. It is important to make forecast of forming imbalances, avert their excessive accumulation, and direct the development of these processes, market conflicts and imbalances into the right course. At the same time it is important to mitigate economic and social side effects of the inevitable and permanent transformation of the economy on a new level.

It is indisputable that improvement of the efficiency of the analysis and forecasting in the macro economy, including monetary, financial, and budget spheres in the balance of trade and balance of payment, adoption of timely adjusting measures will allow avoiding such large scale and destructive crises in the future.

Today forecasting of the situation in the banking sector is fundamental since accrued huge credit risks still threaten the stability of the banking system. Regulatory bodies of many countries conduct stress-testing of the national banking systems. Concurrently, we think that it is important not only to get the results of the stress-testing and forecasting of negative phenomena, but to timely develop a package of measures for recapitalisation of banks and resolve the problems of "toxic assets". Concurrently it is important to adopt amendments in legislation, normative regulatory documents, create relevant institutes (for example, on buying out and further work with "bad" assets) and, if necessary, find and ensure reserves of relevant financial and credit resources.

In 2008-2009, national monetary authorities rendered large scale financial and credit support to the economy and banking sector. It will continue further, however, developed countries do not agree over how large such support has to be. True, measures already taken have led to the growth of the budget deficit and public debt in nearly all of the developed countries, and also in many of the developing countries (see Table).

Deficit of the aggregated state budget and public debt in a number of the leading countries, % to GDP

Countries	Balance of the state budget (+ surplus , - deficit)				Public debt			
	2007	2008	2009	2010	2007	2008	2009	2010
USA	-2.9	-6.1	-13.6	-9.7	63.1	70.5	87.0	97.5
Great Britain	-2.6	-5.4	-9.8	-10.9	44.1	51.9	62.7	72.7
Japan	-2.5	-5.6	-9.9	-9.8	187.7	196.3	217.2	227.4
Canada	1.4	0.4	-3.4	-3.6	64.2	63.6	75.4	77.2
European countries	-0.7	-1.8	-5.4	-6.1	65.8	69.1	78.9	85.0
Germany	-0.5	-0.1	-4.7	-6.1	63.6	67.2	79.4	86.6
France	-2.7	-3.4	-6.2	-6.5	63.9	67.3	74.9	80.3
Italy	-1.5	-2.7	-5.4	-5.9	103.5	105.8	115.3	121.1

Comment to the Table:
The Table actually shows the IMF data for 2007 and 2008 and forecasts for 2009 and 2010. Source: World Economic Outlook. Crisis and Recovery. – International Monetary Fund, April 2009.

Such substantial deficit growth of the state budget and public debt is also a systemic risk for the economy. Hence, along with the increase of the current values of these indicators, the developed countries plan to reduce the budget deficit and the deficit of the public debt in the medium term perspective. We consider that the burden on public finances due to the support rendered to the economy and the banking sector significantly grew and further steps in this direction are fraught with potential danger. So, it is obvious that direct financial aid to the economy in the future probably will not expand and the main emphasis will be on structural reforms at the expense of private investments. In this context (reduction of government spending and increase of the private investments) recent initiatives were developed in the US, for example, on buying out problem assets from the financial institutes. The total value of the programme is USD 1 trillion, of which state funds comprise only USD 75-100 billion, and the rest is planned to be generated from the private investments.

Concurrently in compliance with the adopted decisions at the conference of G8 in April 2009 in London, the total amount for the stimulation of the economy will be USD 5 trillion, of which USD 1.1 trillion will be at the disposal of the international organisations. The IMF, in particular, will get USD 750 billion to support global commercial and financial fields, to resume lending and promote economy growth.

The World Bank is starting to play more and more important role in combating the global crisis. The volume of loans extended by the World Bank in 2008-2009 increased by an unprecedented 54% year-on-year, totally upwards of 59 billion). The World Bank has lend money to 767 projects, with the largest resources being allocated for infrastructure development. According to the World Bank data, due to the crisis the number of requests for loans dramatically increased. According to the same source this trend will continue in 2009-2010.

Sizeable financial resources have been allocated to overcome the consequences of the crisis on the regional level also. For example, the EU Support Fund to Central and Eastern European Countries beyond the Euro zone will double, to EUR 50 billion.

Another direction in combating the crisis is the measures for the liquidation of offshore zones and averting the application of the institute of bank confidentiality for illegal transactions, particularly, tax evasion. Recently, the countries included in the special "black" list of OECD have experienced more and more pressure and, perhaps, the era of offshore playing such a key role in a *super-liberalized* global economy will become a thing of the past.

An important direction is the recovery in confidence towards the financial system and its regulation. The following measures might help to resolve this problem, reduce the systemic risks in the banking and financial sectors: removal of contradictions between national and international legislations; involvement of all financial institutions into the effective system of regulation and supervision including hedge-foundations; enhancement of coordination of the regulatory and supervisory bodies on the national and international levels.

As a result of these reforms, the regulatory bodies, as the UK Minister of Finances, Alistair. Darling noted, "will obtain the power that will enable them to efficiently execute their functions. We need to learn lessons from the financial crisis during which bankers were acting as kamikaze and the regulating bodies failed to handle their duties".

We consider that the institutes whose responsibilities are to resolve the problem of informational asymmetry, - rating agencies, credit bureaus, auditing and consulting companies – also need to undergo serious transformation.

Significant changes should also be made in the management of companies and financial institutes. The key here is that alterations made in the priorities of the strategic and tactical development (rejection of short-lived risky benefit, transfer to the long-term and socially responsible investments), developing and implementing adequate internal control and risk management systems, and effecting an increase in the responsibilities of the owners and managers over the outcomes of the financial activities, including linking the system of financial bonuses with established actual performance indicators and benchmarks.

Implementation of a set of successive anti-crisis measures will allow long existing negative tendencies in the economy to be resolved and to create the enabling conditions for a qualitatively new level of activity to be put into place that will bring about sustainable economic growth.

Bibliography

1. **Abalkin L.I.** Challenges of the new century. Moscow, Institute of Economy of the Russian Academy of Sciences, 2001 (in Russian).

2. **Abalkin L.I.** Policy of the economy in transition. Moscow, Finstatinform, 1997(in Russian).

3. **Agenor P.R., Bhandari J.S., Flood R.P.** Speculative Attacks and Models of Balance of Payments Crises, International Monetary Fund, Washington, D.C. 1991.

4. **Akubardia T.** Market system and the government. Tbilisi, 1996 (in Georgian).

5. **Angell W.** Rules, risk and reform: a proposal for the next decade, Board of Governors of the Federal Reserve System, 1991.

6. **Annual report of the National Bank of Georgia for the year of 2003.** Tbilisi. National Bank of Georgia, 2004 (in Georgian).

7. **Archvadze I.** Georgia will not interfere in the parameters of the hard currency. Tbilisi, Mercury, 2000 (in Georgian).

8. **Aristobulo de J.** The roots of banking crises: micro-economic issues and issues of supervision and regulation, Madrid, 1995.

9.   **Asatiani R**. Financial crisis in Georgia and macro-economic regulation of the transit processes. Academy of Economic Sciences of Georgia. Tbilisi, V.1, 2000 (in Georgian).

10. **Aslund G., Dmitriev M.** Economic Reform Versus Rent Seeking, in Russia after Communism, Washington, D.C. Carnegie Endowment for International Peace, 1999.

11. **Avery R., Terrence Belton.** A comparison of risk-based capital and risk-based deposit insurance, Economic review of Federal Bank of Cleveland, 1987

12. **Babaev A.** National bank of Azerbaijan: peculiarities of the monetary management. Banker, 2003, # 2 (in Russian).

13. **Balcerovicz L.** Socialism, Capitalism, Transformation, Budapest, CEU, 1995.

14. **Balcerovicz L.** Poland, 1989-92., in Political Economy of Economic Reform, Washington, D.C. Institute for International Economics, 1994.

15. **Balyozov Z.** The Bulgarian financial crisis of 1996-1997. Bulgarian national bank. Discussion paper, # 7, 1999.

16. **Basaria R.** Public mentality and the problems of establishing market relations in Georgia. Obschestvo i ekonomika, #2, 1998 (in Russian).

17. **Basel committee on regulation and banking supervision.** Core Principles for effective banking supervision. Basel, September, 1997.

18. **Basel committee on regulation and banking supervision.** Essential elements of a statement of co-operation between banking supervisors. Basel, May, 2001.

19. **Bell J. Pain D.L.** Models of key indicators of the banking crisis: critical analysis. Bank of England , Financial Stability Review, 2000.

20. **Bencivenga, Valerie, and Bruce Smith** Deficits, inflation, and the Banking System in Developing Countries. Oxford Economic Papers, October, 1992.

21. **Berg A. Borensztein E.** Full Dollarisation, The Pros and

Cons, Economic Issues 24, International Monetary Fund, Washington, D.C. 2000.

22. **Berg A. Pattilo C.** The Challenge of Predicting Economic crises, Economic Issues 22, International Monetary Fund, Washington, D.C. 2000.

23. **Beridze T.** Shock Therapy or evolutionary transformation: definitions and the reality. " Materials of the international scientific symposium. Tbilisi, Fredrick Ebert Foundation, 1997.

24. **Blanchard O., Dornbush R., Krugman P., Layard R., Summers L.** Reform in Eastern Europe, Cambridge, The MIT Press, 1994.

25. **Boone P., Gomulka S., Layard R.** Emerging from Communism. Lessons from Russia, China and Europe, Cambridge, The MIT Press, 1998.

26. **Boris M.S., Ding W., Noel M.** The evolution of the state-owned banking sector during transition in Central Europe, Europe-Asia studies. Glasgow, 1997, V. 49, # 7.

27. **Boughton J.M.** From Suez to Tequila: The IMF as Crisis Manager, The Economic Journal, V. 110, #461, 2000.

28. **Bradley B., Ferguson N., Krugman P., Roubini N., Soros G**. et al. The Crisis and How to Deal with It. – The New York Review of Books. Volume 56, number 10. June 11, 200

29. **Braginsky S.**V. Credit and monetary policy in Japan. Moscow, Nauka, 1989 (in Russian).

30. **Budget office of the Parliament of Georgia.** Currency crisis. Reasons for devaluation of Georgian lari and anticipated consequences. Tbilisi, 1999 (in Georgian).

31. **Buyske Gail, Vogel Robert.** Hungary's financial system: status and prospects. W., U.S.A., United States Agency for International Development, 1993.

32. **Bzhezinsky Z.** Great Chess Board. Moscow, International Relations, 2000 (in Russian).

33. **Caprio G. Honohan P. Vittas D.** Finacial Sector Policy for developing Countries, The World Bank, Washington, D.C. 2002.

34. **Caprio G.Jr., Hunter W.C., Kaufman G.G., Leipziger D.M.** Preventing Bank Crises: Lessons from Recent Global Bank Failures, Proceeding of a conference cosponsored by the Federal Reserve Bank of Chicago and the Economic Development Institute of the World Bank, The World Bank, Washington, D.C. 1998.

35. **Caprio G.** Safe and Sound Banking in Developing Countries, The World Bank, 1997.

36. **Caprio G., Klingebiel D.** Episodes of systemic and borderline financial crises. The World Bank, 2000.

37. **Caprio G., Klingebiel D.** Episodes of Systemic and Borderline Banking Crises, Managing the Real and Fiscal Effects of Banking Crises, World Bank Discussion Paper #428, The World Bank, Washington, D.C. 2003.

38. **Caprio G., Klingebiel D.** Episodes of Systemic and Borderline Financial Crises, The World Bank, 2000.

39. **Carmela M., Velazquez F., Funck B.** Europea Integratio and Income Convergence. Lessons for Central and Easter European Countries. 2001.

40. **Chekulaev M.V.** Risk management: managing financial risks on the basis of the volatility analysis. Moscow. Alpina publisher, 2002 (in Russian).

41. **Chikava L.** Market economy: problem of social controversies. Obschestvo i ekonomika, #1, 1998 (in Russian).

42. **Chikava L.** Social disorientation of the Georgian economy and its defining factors. Academy of Economic Sciences of Georgia. Tbilisi, V.1, 2000 (in Georgian).

43. **Chitanava N.** About state regulation of the economy (methodological approach). Academy of Economic Sciences of Georgia. Tbilisi, V.1, 2000 (in Georgian).

44. **Chitanava N.** Social-economic problems of the transitional

period (economic globalisation and national-economic security). Tbilisi, Part III, 2001 (in Georgian).

45. **Claessens S., Klingebiel D., Leaven L.** Financial restructuring in Banking and Corporate Sector Crises: Which Policies to Pursue?, Managing the Real and Fiscal Effects of Banking Crises, World Bank Discussion Paper #428, The World Bank, Washington, D.C. 2003.

46. **Debelle G., Masson P., Savastano M., Sharma S.** Inflation targeting as a Framework for Monetary policy, Economic Issues 15, International Monetary Fund, Washington, D.C. 1998.

47. Deutche Bundesbank. Monatsbericht. Dezember 2002.

48. **Dostalek F.** Das tschechische Bankwesen. – Bank, Kuln, # 7, 1998.

49. **Dziobek C., Pazarbaşioğlu C.** Lessons from Systemic Bank restructuring, Economic Issues 14, International Monetary Fund, Washington, D.C. 1998.

50. **Easterly W.** The Lost Decades: Developing Countries Stagnation. Spite of Policy Reform 1980-1998, February, 2001.

51. **EBRD** Annual report 1998, London, 1999.

52. **EBRD** Annual report 1999, London, 2000.

53. **EBRD** Annual report 2000, London, 2001.

54. **EBRD** Annual report 2001, London, 2002.

55. **EBRD** Annual report 2002, London, 2003.

56. **EBRD** Annual report 2003, London, 2004.

57. **EBRD** Annual report 2004, London, 2005.

58. **EBRD** Annual report 2005, London, 2006.

59. **EBRD** Annual report 2006, London, 2007.

60. **EBRD** Annual report 2007, London, 2008.

61. **EBRD** Annual report 2008, London, 2009.

62. **EBRD**. Principles and regulations for purchasing goods and services. London, 2000. (in Russian).

63. **EBRD,** EBRD investments 1991-2001, London, 2002.

64. **EBRD,** EBRD: The first ten years of a new generation bank, volume 1, London, 2001.

65. **EBRD,** Financing with the EBRD, London, 2002.

66. **EBRD,** Natural Resources, London, 2001.

67. **EBRD,** The EBRD: its role and activities, London, 1999.

68. **Edison H.J., Luangaram P., Miller M.,** Asset Bubbles, Domino Effects and 'Lifeboats': Elements of the East Asian Crisis, 1998 (http://www.cepr.org/pubs/new-dps/dplist. asp?dpno=1866).

69. **Eichengreen B., Rose A., Wyplosz C.** Contagious Currency Crises, NBER Working Paper, Cambridge, #5681, 1996.

70. **Enoch C., Gulde, A-M., Hardy D**. Banking Crises and Bank Resolution: Experiences in Some Transition Economies, International Monetary Fund, Washington, D.C. 2002.

71. **Fleming Alex, Lily Chu, Marie-Renee Bakker** The Baltics-Banking Crises Observed. Policy Research Working Paper 1647. World Bank, Washington, 1996.

72. **Fleming Alex, Samuel Talley** The Latvian Banking Crisis: Lessons Learned. Policy Research Working Paper 1590. World Bank, Washington, 1996.

73. **Flood R.P., Marion N.P.** A Model of the Joint Distribution of Banking and Exchange-Rate Crises, International Monetary Fund, Washington, D.C. 2001.

74. **Fontela E**. The era of finance. – Futures. Guildford, 1998. Vol.30, № 8

75. **Forum of financial stability.** A guide to the development of efficient systems for the deposit insurance. Basel, September, 2001.

76. **Gaidar E.** Anomalies of economic growth. Moscow, Finstatinform, 1997 (in Russian).

77. **Gamsakhurdia G., Kovzanadze I.** Reliability and sustainability of the commercial banks. Gadasakhadebi. Tbilisi, #6, 2000 (in Georgian).

78. **Gamsakhurdia G.** To the issue of key directions of the monetary policy of Georgia. Macro Micro Economics. Tbilisi, #3, 1998 (in Georgian).

79. **Garber P.M.** Derivative products in exchange rate crises, 1998.

80. **Garcia G.G.** Protecting Bank Deposits, Economic Issues 9, International Monetary Fund, 1997.

81. **Garcia G.G.** Deposit insurance; research in the current systems and the best practices. International Monetary Fund, Washington, D.C. 1999, (in Russian).

82. Georgia, Economic Update and Strategies for Reform, Prepared by the World Bank for the Consultative Group Meeting for Georgia, October 21, 1994.

83. **Ghudushauri L.** Credit and current banking mechanism. Tbilisi, Tbilisi University Press, 1998 (in Georgian).

84. **Giannini C.** Enemy of none but a common friend of all? An international perspective on the lender of last resort function, Temi di discussione: Banca d'Itallia, № 341, Roma, 1998.

85. **Gogokhia R.K.** On the issue of the mixed economic system in the process of formation of the global economy. Academy of Economic Sciences of Georgia. Tbilisi, V.2, 2001 (in Georgian).

86. Global Financial Stability Report. - International Monetary Fund, April 2009

87. **Gotsiridze R., Kandelaki O.** Influential groups and corruption: threat to the National security of Georgia. Tbilisi, 2001 (in Georgian).

88. **Grishikashvili A.** Countries in transition: problems and prospects. Tbilisi, 1998 (in Georgian).

89. **Guillen, Mauro F.** The Limits of Convergence. Globalisation

and Organisational Change in Argentina, South Korea and Spain. - Princeton University Press, 2001.

90. **Gupta S., Clements B., Macdonald K., Shiller K.** IMF and poverty problems. Budgetary issues management. Washington: IMF, 1998, a series of brochures, #52 (in Russian).

91. **Gurgenidze L., Lobzhanidze M., Onoprishvili D.** Georgia: Planning to Hyperinflation, Communist Economies & Economic Transformation, Vol. 6, #2, 1994.

92. **Gvelesiani R.** Regulation of economy: untraditional methods. SRI of economic and social problems. Tbilisi, V. 4, 1999 (in Georgian).

93. **Hanson J. Honohan P. Majnoni G.** Globalisation and National Systems, A copublication of the World Bank and Oxford University Press, The World Bank, Washington, D.C. 2003.

94. **Heffernan Sh.** Modern Banking in Theory and Practice, London, 1999.

95. **Honohan P., Klingebiel D.** Controlling the Fiscal Costs of Banking Crises, Managing the Real and Fiscal Effects of Banking Crises, World Bank Discussion Paper #428, The World Bank, Washington, D.C. 2003.

96. **Horchicova M.** The old loans problem: the Czech experience. Eastern European economics, V.35, #2, 1997.

97. Hungary: foreign banks welcome. Banker, L., 1997, # 851

98. **IBRD,** Lessons of Tax Reform, The World Bank, Washington, D.C. 1991.

99. **IMF,** A Study of the Soviet Economy, V. 3, IMF, IBRD, OECD, EBRD, Paris, OECD, 1991.

100. **IMF,** Georgia: Tax Policy review, Washington D.C. IMF, 2000.

101. **IMF,** International Financial Statistics, Washington D.C. IMF, 2001.

102. **IMF,** The Information Technology Revolution, World Economic outlook, Washington D.C. IMF, 2001.

103. **IMF,** SDR Valuation, http://www.imf.org, June.

104. **Jgerenaia E.** The issues of genesis of the monetary reform in Georgia. Macro Micro Economics. Tbilisi, #9, 2000 (in Georgian).

105. **Jibuti M.** The latest history and prospects of integrations of Georgian economy into the world economy. TSU, Tbilisi, Issue XVI, 2001 (in Georgian).

106. **Julakidze G.** The issues of improvement of the financial system in the transitional period. Tbilisi, 1999 (in Georgian).

107. **Kakulia M.** Currency crisis of 1998-1999 in Georgia. Proceedings of the Academy of Science of Georgia. Tbilisi, #34, V.8, 2001 (in Georgian).

108. **Kakulia M.** Problems of currency system development in Georgia. Tbilisi, 2001(in Georgian).

109. **Kakulia R.** Monetary system reform. Obschestvo i ekonomika.1998. #2, pp131-135 (in Russian).

110. **Kern H.** Die Bankensysteme der Tschechischen und Slowakischen Republic. Regensburg, 1997, Kap.1.

111. **Khachatrian A.** Paradox of Armenian economy. Informational-analytical review of the Agency Eurasianet of 07.01.2002, (in Russian).

112. **Khelaia G.** International currency, credit and settlement relations.Tbilisi, Lampari, 1996 (in Georgian).

113. **Khelaia G.** Some vital issues of money circulation and credit. Tbilisi, Lampari , 1993 (in Georgian).

114. **Kistauri L.** National Bank (formation, activities, future). Tbilisi, 1996 (in Georgian).

115. **Kistauri Sh.**, **Kistauri L.** Problems of financial and banking law in Georgia.Tbilisi, 1997 (in Georgian).

116. **Kommersant.** 2003, 26 February.

117. Kontridze G. Deposit insurance system and its applying perspectives in Georgia. PhD thesis, Tbilisi, Tbilisi State University. 2006 (in Georgian).

118. **Kormendi R., Snyder E.** Bank privatisation in transitional economies, The William Davidson Institute at the University of Michigan business School, 1996.

119. **Kovzanadze I.** About the stability of the banking system. Bulletin of the Academy of Science of Georgia.Tbilisi, V. 9, #4, 2001. (in Georgian).

120. **Kovzanadze I.** About the system of financial coefficients of complex assessment of the activities of the commercial banks. Georgian engineering news. Tbilisi, 2000, #3, pp. 173-179.

121. **Kovzanadze I.** Capital adequacy – a key element of the sustainability of a commercial bank. Bankovskoe delo. Moscow, 2001, #12, pp.5-8 (in Russian).

122. **Kovzanadze I.** Currency and financial mechanism of the countries with developing market economies under condition of globalisation. Financi i credit. Moscow, 2004, #23, pp.40-47.(in Russian).

123. **Kovzanadze I.** Development of the competitive environment of the banking market. Auditor, Moscow, 2000, #12, pp. 30-32 (in Russian).

124. **Kovzanadze I.**Economic and Banking system development trends and prospects for countries in transition. Moscow, Finansi i statistika, 2005

125. **Kovzanadze I.** Factoring transactions: types, regulation, accounting and profit analysis. Dengi i kredit, Moscow, 2001, #11, pp.17-20 (in Russian).

126. **Kovzanadze I.** Financial sphere: the ways for overcoming the crisis. Economist, Moscow, 2003, #6, pp. 33-36 (in Russian).

127. **Kovzanadze I.** Liquidity as a Criterion of Bank Management. Bulletin of the Georgian Academy of Sciences, Tbilisi, V. 10, 2002, #3-4 (in Georgian).

128. **Kovzanadze I.** Modern approaches to the problem of development and provisions of stability of the banking system. Bugalteria i banki. Moscow, 2000, #12, pp. 4-8 (in Russian).

129. **Kovzanadze I.** Monetary and credit policy under conditions of systemic banking crises: national and international aspects. Dengi i kredit. Moscow, 2003, #2, pp45-47 (in Russian)

130. **Kovzanadze I.** On the issue of defining the concept of the liquidity. Proceedings of the Georgian Academy of Sciences. Tbilisi, 2000, V. 9, #3, pp.109-122 (in Georgian).

131. **Kovzanadze I.** On the issue of improvement of providing the economy with credit resources. Macro Micro Economics. Tbilisi, #4, 2000 (in Georgian).

132. **Kovzanadze I.** On the methods for managing the problem banks. Finansi i kredit. Moscow, 2001, #16, pp. 78-80 (in Russian).

133. **Kovzanadze I.** Peculiarities of the development of the banking systems of the former socialistic countries. Voprosi ekonomiki, Moscow, 2004, #5, pp.135-141 (in Russian).

134. **Kovzanadze I.** Problems of functioning of the commercial banks of Georgia on the current stage . Tbilisi, Tbilisi University Press, 2001 (in Georgian).

135. **Kovzanadze I.** Problems of improvement of the investment activities of the commercial banks of Georgia. Banki, Tbilisi. 2000, #4, pp. 20-26 (in Georgian).

136. **Kovzanadze I.** Regulation of liquidity of the credit organisations by the central bank. Bugalteria i banki, Moscow, 2001, #11, pp. 28-31 (in Russian).

137. **Kovzanadze I.** Restructuring of the banking systems: strategy and tactics of overcoming systemic crises. Financi, Moscow, 2003, #3, pp. 72-74 (in Russian).

138. **Kovzanadze I.** Role of the bank deposits insurance system in ensuring economic and social stability. Bulletin of the Georgian Academy of Sciences, Tbilisi, 164, #2, 2001, p. 407-409.

139. **Kovzanadze I**. Role of the commercial banks in strengthening the banking system. Macro Micro Economics, Tbilisi, 2000, #7-8, pp. 51-52 (in Georgian).

140. **Kovzanadze I**. Some problems of transition of the banks to the international standards of financial accounting. Economist, Moscow, 2002, #10, pp.43-46, (in Russian).

141. **Kovzanadze I**. Some questions about the development of the competitive banking market. Bankovskoe delo, Moscow, 2001, #4, pp.41-46 (in Russian).

142. **Kovzanadze I**. Systemic banking crises under condition of financial globalisation. Voprosi ekonomiki, Moscow, 2002, #8, pp. 89-101 (in Russian).

143. **Kovzanadze I**. Systemic banking crises under conditions of financial globalisation. Tbilisi, Tbilisi University Press, 2003 (in Russian).

144. **Kovzanadze I**. The issues of formation of the effective system for managing banking risks. Dengi i kredit, Moscow, 2001, #3, pp.49-53.

145. **Kovzanadze I**. Some aspects of Problem Banks management, Economic and Business, Tbilisi, #5, 2008 (in Georgian).

146. **Kovzanadze I**. Economic and Banking System Development Trends and Prospects for Countries in Transition, iUniverse Inc., New York, Bloomington, 2008.

147. **Kovzanadze I. Kontridze G**. Some problems of Georgian Banking system before august 2008 events, Georgian Economic, Tbilisi, #1, 2009 (in Georgian).

148. **Krugman P,** Analytical Afterthoughts On the Asian Crisis, December 9, 1999 (http://web.mit.edu/krugman/www/MINICRIS.htm).

149. **Krugman P.** Retour sur le krach asiatique. – Expansion. P, 1998, # 571.

150. **Krugman P.** Currency Crises, Chicago, University of Chicago Press, 2000.

151. **Krugman P., Obstfeld M.** International Economy. Theory and policy. SPb. Peter, 2003.

152. **Kunert J.** Bankovni sector Ceske Republiku, Econom. Pr., 1998, # 27.

153. **Makarevich L.** Crisis of post-soviet banking system. Moscow. Analytical Centre of Financial Information, 1998 (in Russian).

154. **Managadze I.** Crucial – to maintain stable prices, low inflation growth. – Interview to the Ukrainian magazine "Bankir" 2003, #3 (in Russian).

155. **Martin Carmela, Francisco J. Velazquez, Bernard Funck.** Europea Integratio and Income Convergence. Lessons for Central and Easter Europea Countries. 2001.

156. **Martin G.P., Schumann X.** Western globalisation. Moscow, Alpina, 2001.

157. **Matuk G.** Financial systems in France and other countries. Moscow, Finstatinform, 1994(in Russian).

158. **Mauro P.** Why Worry about Corruption, Economic Issues 6, International Monetary Fund, Washington, D.C. 1997.

159. **Mekhrjakov V.** Banking system in Russia: current situation and development problems.Voprosi ekonomiki, 1995, #11, pp.11-15 (in Russian).

160. **Mekvabishvili E.** Influence of the economic growth and globalisation on the monetary and credit policy of Georgia. Banki, Tbilisi, 2000, #2, pp.3-7 (in Georgian).

161. **Mekvabishvili E.** The state and the economy. Tbilisi, Tbilisi University Press, 1996 (in Georgian).

162. **Meskhia I., Murjikneli M.** Economic reform in Georgia (analysis, directions, problems).Tbilisi, TSU, 1996 (in Georgian).

163. **Meskhia I.** External and internal factors of the financial stabilisation in Georgia. Tbilisi, Siaxle, 2000 (in Georgian).

164. **Michel Van De Velde.** Introduction of the international

accounting standards into the commercial banks of Georgia. Banki, 2000, #1, pp.38-42 (in Georgian).

165. **Miller L.R., Van-Hus D.D**. Modern money and banking business. Moscow, Infra-M, 2000 (in Russian).

166. **Miller M., Zhang L.** Sovereign Liquidity Crises: the Strategic Case for a Payments Standstill, 1999 (http://www.warwick.ac.uk/fac/soc/CSGR/current/rbws4.pdf).

167. **Minassian G.** The road to economic disaster in Bulgaria, Europe-Asia studies, 1998, V.50, # 2.

168. **Montes M.**F., **Popov V.V.** Asian virus or Dutch malady? Theory and practice of currency crises in Russia and other countries. Moscow, Delo, 2000 (in Russian).

169. **Montes-Negret F., Papi L.** The Polish experience with Bank and enterprise restructuring, The World Bank. Washington, 1997.

170. **Moskvin V.**A. Are large banks reliable? Biznes i banki, 1996, #36, pp. 10-13 (in Russian).

171. **Papava V.** About formation of the economic system in Southern Caucasus.Obschestvo i ekonomika, #1, 2001 (in Russian).

172. **Papava V.** Impact of inflation on the economic growth in the post-soviet Georgia. Banki, #1, 2000 (in Georgian).

173. **Papava V.** Political economy of the post-communist capitalism and economy of Georgia. Tbilisi, 2002 (in Georgian).

174. **Provkin I.**I. Investments in the real sector of economy: Role of banks. Dengi i kredit, #3, pp. 44-47, 2001 (in Russian).

175. **Reed E.** Commercial banks. Moscow, Progress, 1990 (in Russian).

176. **Roze P.**S. Bank management. Moscow, Delo, 1995 (in Russian).

177. Republic of Georgia, Statement of Economic Policies, September 18, 1994.

178. Republic of Georgia, Use of Fund Resources – Request for Purchase under the Systemic Transformation Facility, Document of International Monetary Fund, December 1, 1994.

179. Republic of Georgia, Use of Fund Resources – Request for Purchase under the Systemic Transformation Facility, Document of International Monetary Fund, EBS/95/101, June 15, 1995.

180. Review of the economic stance of Europe. Geneva. UN. 2000, #1 (in Russian).

181. **Sachs J.** International economics: Unlocking the mysteries of globalisation. Foreign policy, N.Y., 1998, # 110.

182. **Santeladze N.** Economy reform and formation of a new social and economic model in Georgia. Academy of Economic Sciences of Georgia. Tbilisi, V. 3, 2001 (in Georgian).

183. **Scharrer E.-M.** Stahn Ch. Skandinavische banken im Fussionsfieber. Bank, Koln, 1998, # 11.

184. **Severino J.-M.** Le dialogue entre les institutions de Bretton-Woods et les banques est essentiel. Banque, # 593, 1998.

185. **Sevruk V.T**. Bank risks. Moscow, Delo, 1995 (in Russian).

186. **Shatirishvili D**. Actual questions of improvement of the banking reforms. Messenger of the Georgian Academy of Sciences. Tbilisi, V. 3-4, 1997, pp.29-41 (in Georgian).

187. **Shiller R.J.** The new financial order, risk in the 21st century. Princeton University Press, 2003.

188. **Shokhin A.N. Social problems of perestroika.** Moscow, 1989 (in Russian).

189. **Silagadze A.** Some issues of privatisation of the state property in Georgia. Materials from international scientific symposium. Tbilisi, Frederick Ebert Foundation, 1997 (in Georgian).

190. **Silagadze A.** Social- economic issue of privatisation of the state property in Georgia. Obschestvo i ekonomika, 1998, #2.

191. **Sinki J**. M. Finance management in the commercial banks. Moscow, Gatallaxy, 1994 (in Russian).

192. **Social and economic situation in Georgia**. State Department of Statistics of Georgia. Tbilisi, 2001.

193. **Stigliz J.E.** From miracle to crisis to recovery. Lessons from four decades of East Asian experience. Stigliz J.E. and Yusuf S. Rethinking the East Asian miracle, Washington, DC, and New York: World Bank and Oxford University Press,2001.

194. **Stiglitz J.E.** Globalisation: alarming trends. Moscow, 2003.

195. **Stiglitz J.E.** Globalisation and its Discontents, New York, 2002.

196. **Stiglitz J.E.** The World Bank at the Millennium. The Economic Journal, V. 109, #459, 1999.

197. **Stiglitz J.E.** Where do reforms take us? (To the tenth anniversary of the beginning of the transitional processes). Issues of economics, #7, 1999.

198. The Georgian Business Week, 2003-2004.

199. The Federal Reserve of Board. www.federalreserve.gov

200. **Tissen F., Gisher X.** Credit transactions. Basel II and the costs of banks refinancing. Kreditwesen, #12, 2002.

201. **Tsereteli G.** The basis of economic-mathematical methods and some of the practical aspects of their application. Tbilisi, Mecniereba, 1999 (in Georgian).

202. **Tsereteli G.** Methodological basis for mathematical modelling of economy and practical examples of its application. Tbilisi, Mecniereba, 2000 (in Georgian).

203. Turkish Daily News, 05.01.2002.

204. **Wang Jian-ye** The Georgian Hyperinflation and Stabilisation, IMF Working Paper, International Monetary Fund, Washington, D.C. 1999.

205. **Wolf T. Gurgen E.** Improving Governance and Fighting Corruption in the Baltic and CIS Countries, The Role of

the IMF, Economic Issues 21, International Monetary Fund, Washington, D.C. 2000.

206. **Wolfenson J.D.** The Challenge of Inclusion, Address to the Board of Governors, Hong Kong, China, September 23, Washington D.C., The World Bank, 1999.

207. **Wolfenson J.D.** The Other Crisis of Inclusion, Address to the Board of Governors, Washington D.C., October 6, Washington D.C., The World Bank, 1998.

208. **Wolfenson J.D.** A Proposal for a Comprehensive Development Framework (A discussion Draft), Washington D.C., The World Bank, 1999.

209. **Wolfenson J.D.** Coalitions for Change, Address to the Board of Governors, Washington D.C., September 28, Washington D.C., The World Bank, 1999.

210. **Wolfson M.** Transitions from a command Economy: Rational Expectations and Cold Turkey, Contemporary Policy Issues, V. 10, April, 1992.

211. **Woo D.** Two Approaches to Resolving Nonperforming Assets During Financial Crises, International Monetary Fund, Washington, D.C. 2000.

212. **World Bank.** Bureaucrats in business. Economics and politics of government ownership. Washington: World Bank, 2001.

213. **World Bank.** From plan to market. World development report, 1996, Oxford, 1996.

214. **World Bank.** Attacking poverty. World development report 2000/2001. Moscow, 2001 (in Russian).

215. World Economic Outlook. Crisis and Recovery. – International Monetary Fund, April 2009

216. Workbook on regulation of supervision over the activities of the commercial banks. Tbilisi, 1999 (in Georgian).

217. **Yersuk L.** National Bank of Lithuania – strengthening bank supervision. Washington, 1997.

www.ingramcontent.com/pod-product-compliance
Lightning Source LLC
Chambersburg PA
CBHW030005190526
45157CB00014B/429